THE 233D ENGINEER COMBAT BATTALION

THE 233D ENGINEER COMBAT BATTALION
1943-1945

BY

VICTOR E. WEAVER

SERGEANT MICHAEL J. RAWLINGS

TECHNICIAN FOURTH GRADE HAROLD J. KIPFMILLER

SERGEANT STANLEY C. HAHULA

PRIVATE FIRST CLASS THEODORE P. HAGSTROM

CORPORAL PATRICK H. DONAHUE

TECHNICIAN FIFTH GRADE JEROME J. BARNETT

TECHNICIAN FIFTH GRADE GEORGE HUTCHINGS

FIRST EDITION

MARCH, 1947

The 233d Engineer Combat Battalion 1943-1945 is part of the
UNCOMMON VALOR REPRINT SERIES

Printed in the United States of America

UNCOMMON VALOR SERIES EDITION
ISBN: 979-8869036322

THIS BOOK IS DEDICATED TO

PRIVATE HARRY A. JOHNSON

TECHNICIAN FIFTH GRADE ANTHONY L. COCUZZO

TECHNICIAN FIFTH GRADE ROY A. KILLAM

STAFF SERGEANT HARRY E. McDANIEL

PRIVATE GILBERT T. OWENS

PRIVATE RICHARD H. FORBES

PRIVATE LLOYD W. SHELLENBARGER

SERGEANT MICHAEL J. RAWLINGS

TECHNICIAN FOURTH GRADE HAROLD J. KIPFMILLER

SERGEANT STANLEY C. HAHULA

PRIVATE FIRST CLASS THEODORE P. HAGSTROM

CORPORAL PATRICK H. DONAHUE

TECHNICIAN FIFTH GRADE JEROME J. BARNETT

TECHNICIAN FIFTH GRADE GEORGE HUTCHINGS

CONTENTS

ACKNOWLEDGMENT

Thanks are given to all the men and officers of the Battalion for their consideration and help in preparing the material for this History.

To Sheldon J. Shalett, especially, goes much credit for the hours he spent on Okinawa and in Japan collecting, compiling and writing much of the material used. Full credit is due him for the compilation of correct dates and statistics on moves, the basic outline of the sequence of events, the compilation of rosters, and all statistics from the Battalion's files and reports used in writing this book.

Much of the credit for the statistics used in the earlier chapters of the book on the training of the Battalion is due Lieutenant Thomas G. Blair. Lieutenant Blair was the Battalion Adjutant, on the staffs of Lieutenant Colonel Clayton S. Gates and Lieutenant Colonel Alexander W. Jurvic, and the journals he kept were most valuable to the author.

To Captain Clarence E. Johnson and Chief Warrant Officer George Lucas go thanks for their assistance in recalling details of incidents depicted herein.

To Captain Theodore C. Meinelt and the Battalion photographers, Technicians Fifth Grade Robert K. Mika and Jack E. Koster, is due the credit for all photographs and maps used in the History unless otherwise designated. Much of the material used was from the files of the S-2 Section.

Thanks are extended to Lieutenant Peter J. Langhans for his help in recording some of the incidents related in the book, and for the use of pictures from his own personal library, so indicated.

We are grateful to the editorial staff of the *Infantry Journal*, for their generous help in the proofreading and correcting of the manuscript and assistance in assembling and laying out the book.

V. E. W.

INTRODUCTION

The news stories all glorified the famous "End Run" to the assault landing on enemy-held beaches three miles south of Ormoc, Leyte, Philippine Islands.

Time magazine, December 18, 1944, put it this way:

BATTLE OF THE PACIFIC

General Bruce—Sevens for the 77th.

Before dawn on the 7th, the 225-mile end run from Leyte Gulf, through Surigao Strait and up into the Camotes Sea, had been completed. Almost a hundred craft under Rear Admiral Dewey Struble, a Normandy veteran, lay off shore. At 6:30 the destroyers opened up on the beaches with 5-inch guns; after 20 minutes, LCIs carrying rocket launchers belched their loads onto a 12,000-yard beachhead. At 0707 (because General Bruce likes sevens for his 77th) the first troops sloshed up the beaches, without a casualty. . . . Within three hours, the ships were unloaded and beginning to pull out. The Jap air force struck, with substantial numbers, but in small groups. . . . Only after nine hours were the Japs finally driven off. But they had done some damage.

One flaming Jap plane flew five miles before it crashed into a U. S. Destroyer. Another destroyer was torpedoed and sunk; an APD was sunk. The crews were rescued. . . . Once ashore, the 77th made rapid progress. It overran Camp Downs, and from that plateau rolled downhill with momentum unchecked, entering Ormoc at week's end. The end run had produced a touchdown. The 77th now held the vital position on the west coast of Leyte; the position could serve as an anvil while other U. S. Divisions, like hammers, pounded the Japs caught between.

Weeks later the clipping came in the mail; the fellows read it, passed it around. Other newspaper clippings arrived; the folks back home were reading about it.

"That's us," remarked a mud-laden engineer.

"Yes, I guess the folks will know; they know we're with the 77th."

Although their story was far from being told in its entirety, they were satisfied. As long as the folks back home knew about them they didn't especially mind what had passed or what was to come. They felt that some day when, or if, they got home, the entire story would be told.

That is the purpose of this book—to tell a story, the story of the men of the 233d Engineer Combat Battalion . . . their combat experiences, the story they want to be told. It comprises the better part of the history, and in its writing it is fully realized that at its best this book will be only a brief summary of the full story.

Each act of heroism or determination, each recording of skill and self-sacrifice, and each feat of bravery depicted will be only one of many. Throughout the entire writing of this book I have had to be content with the telling of a few incidents with the full certainty of neglecting many. The only records of many acts of courage are still being held in the hearts of the doers, and only because they were seen by someone else did those related here become known. For it was the spirit of the Battalion that to sacrifice, to go beyond the call of duty and to accomplish the job at any cost was merely doing the job well.

If this book tells the story they want told, if it brings a feeling of pride to the members of the Battalion, if it brings enjoyment to its readers, it will have fulfilled its purpose, and it is further hoped that in its recording I have brought forth the spirit of undying cooperation that so successfully carried the 233d Engineers across the many beaches in the Pacific Theater and made the accomplishment of their every mission possible.

VICTOR E. WEAVER.

PART ONE
THE NARRATIVE

CHAPTER 1

IN THE BEGINNING

The 2d Battalion of the 348th Engineer Regiment (General Service) was constituted in the Organized Reserve on the 29th of July, 1921. On the 1st of January, 1938 it was withdrawn from the Reserve and made an inactive unit of the Regular Army, and on the 15th of July, 1942 was activated at Camp Crowder, Missouri. The Regiment consisted of a regimental headquarters, two battalions of three companies each, and a headquarters detachment. Major Clayton S. Gates assumed command and conducted initial schools and training for the officers.

On the 21st of August, 1942 Colonel Sylvester E. Nortner assumed command, and the unit engaged in usual garrison duties and the training of cadre and officers. On the 1st of September, 1942 after receiving about four hundred fillers the 13-week mobilization training program was put into effect.

The first move for the new Regiment came on the 29th of October, 1942. This was a rail movement to the Desert Training Center, Camp Young, California. Upon its arrival, the 3d of November, 1942, the unit was stationed at Freda, California. Normal MTP training followed and the regiment also built roads and camp sites for other units arriving for desert training.

Two months later, the 6th of January, 1943, the 2d Battalion departed by train en route to Camp Pendleton, Virginia, arriving there on the 12th of January. At this time Major Clayton S. Gates was the Battalion commander. The unpacking and reorganization had scarcely been completed when this battalion was redesignated the 233d Engineer Combat Battalion and activated. This was the beginning of the long, hazardous road to the Japanese homeland.

But first, the Battalion needed further training, and for this the unit moved to Fort Story, Virginia.

Here the Battalion was assigned to the Eastern Defense Command, attached to the Chesapeake Bay Sector, and further attached to the Mobile Force, Chesapeake Bay Sector, which was the 111th Regimental Combat Team under the command of Colonel Skelton. These numerous headquarters in the chain of command each required copies of all paper work and it was here that the mimeograph machine came into its own. On the 22d of February, 1943 Major Gates was promoted to the grade of Lieutenant Colonel and the Battalion began to shape up with Lieutenant Norman G. Crumpecker, Lieutenant Eugene E. Skogerson, Lieutenant Robert H. Sayre and Lieutenant Robert K. Graham commanding H&S, A, B and C Companies, respectively. The Battalion was then split up, and each line company was sent to defensive positions in the Chesapeake Bay Sector. Company A was attached to the 1st Battalion of the 111th Infantry, along with Battery A, 176th Field Artillery, at Camp Somerset, Westover, Maryland. Company B went to Camp Ashby, Thalia, Virginia, with the 3d Battalion, 111th Infantry, and Battery C, 176th Field Artillery. Company C was attached to the 2d Battalion, 111th Infantry, with Battery B, 176th Field Artillery, at Camp Battle, New Bern, North Carolina. Battalion Headquarters and H&S Company remained at Fort Story.

This deviation from the normal training of a unit, where the sub-units work together hand-in-hand, created a feeling of independence within the various companies. It was still the 233d Engineer Combat Battalion, but at Camp Battle the emphasis was more apt to be on Company C of the 233d; on Company A of the 233d at Camp Somerset, or on Company B of the 233d at Camp Ashby. A more intense feeling of competition arose between the companies and the *esprit* of each grew steadily. Each, within itself, attempted to become outstanding and when the final count was taken this individual competitive spirit was reflected in the performance of *the* Battalion. For here was proof of the statement that a unit is only as good as its component parts.

During March 308 recruits arrived at Fort Story to take their basic training. This completed the roster of the Battalion. The bulk of the new arrivals came from the Middle West, from such camps as Fort Sheridan, Illinois; Camp Custer, Michigan; Jefferson Barracks, Missouri; Scott Field, Illinois; Fort Leavenworth, Kansas, and Fort Snelling, Minnesota. They were formed into five training platoons, the first commanded by Lieutenant William D. Mitchell, the second by Lieutenant Henry A. Lind, the third by Lieutenant Harley T. Crawford, the fourth by Lieutenant Max L. Daley, and the fifth by Lieutenant William W. Lassetter. Corporal Duane D. Vegors, Corporal Earl G. Fessler, Sergeant Archie M. Reed, Corporal Arthur B. Charbonnel, and Corporal Robert F. Pooler were the respective platoon sergeants.

During the latter part of March these platoons began basic training, and for the next two weeks the gravel motor pool at Fort Story resounded to the sound of marching feet and oral commands.

"Right step . . . hhhhoooorch! To the rear . . . hhhhoooorch!

Parts of squads drifting off by themselves were common sights, as were the exasperated platoon sergeants trying to chase down the remnants of a platoon after a "first-squad-to-the-rear-march-second-squad-to-the-rear-march," maneuver. At the end of the first two weeks, however, the "rookies" were making a satisfactory showing on the parade ground, and the effects of their training was becoming noticeable. After close-order drill came extended order, more suited to field maneuvers.

The scrub-covered sand dunes behind camp proved an ideal training ground of hills and valleys, for "ambushes," antiaircraft defense, gas-attack drill and infantry problems in general. A number of the men were beginning to show aptitude for special jobs and were selected to attend various training schools. Privates John A. Bickford, John N. Schavilje, Sheldon J. Shalett, Douglas A. Kohl, Donald C. Allensworth, William C. Friday and William E. Noack were sent to the communications school at Fort Monroe, Virginia, conducted by the 111th Infantry. Later they were to round out the communications section of the Battalion. About this same time Merrill E. Blackman and Harvey J. Field were attending the Engineer's Enlisted Specialist School at the University of Kentucky at Lexington. Blackman, attending a course in surveying, was later to become the Battalion Operations Sergeant, and Field, attending a course in topographical drafting, was to become the Battalion Intelligence Sergeant.

After a brief introduction to Infantry tactics, on April 13 the recruits began a two-month training period as Combat Engineers. Bridges were built and torn down, demolitions were constantly exploding; the woods surrounding the camp were dotted with road blocks, tank traps, weapon emplacements, firing ranges, infiltration courses and more bridges. There were more demolitions and more work and more training until on the 4th of June, 1943 these "rookies"—no longer rookies—were ready to take their place as trained combat engineers among the men of the different companies of the Battalion.

Lt. Lassetter's platoon finished on top of the list at the end of this basic period, with Private Donald A. Thompson in first place

These men were finding out they could shoot.

with an "expert" score of 191. Private Harold Arnenson, score 188, and Private Anton L. Kasprovicz, score 187, were runners-up. These men were not only finding out that they could learn to be engineers, but also that they could shoot.

Schools were still in order, for many specialists are needed in a combat engineer outfit. Private John H. Foster was sent to Washington and Jefferson College in Washington, Pennsylvania, for a course in Army Classification. Private Charlie Williams went to Fort Belvoir, Virginia, to attend a Water Purification and Distillation Course.

The Battalion was destined never to stay for long in any one place, and the members were beginning to realize this. On the 14th of July, 1943 another movement began. The various units of the Battalion, from their scattered stations, began to move to the location of the MFCBS maneuvers in North Carolina. Company A left Camp Somerset to meet H&S and Battalion Headquarters, and at Dover Range, Virginia, radio contact was made. H&S and Headquarters was already on the move. Shortly thereafter the units merged into a single convoy and were on their way. It was an impressive sight as the almost one hundred trucks, air compressors, jeeps, command cars, trailers with dozers mounted,

Radio gave the Battalion Commander control over the convoy.

and all the other equipment of the Battalion rolled at thirty-five miles an hour over the highways of Virginia and North Carolina. Guards from the Battalion were posted at all railroad crossings and at all intersections in towns and cities along the route. The kitchens functioned, preparing the meals in the rolling kitchen trucks and serving the men at short prearranged stops. Radio gave the Battalion Commander control over the convoy. At New Bern, Company C joined the convoy, and on the 15th of July the Mobile Forces, Chesapeake Bay Sector were assembled at Croatan National Forest, North Carolina, for the coming two-week maneuver period.

At this point began one of the Battalion's traditional hexes, one that followed them all the way through to VJ-day—*rain*. On the 15th of July the rains came, and on every move thereafter they never failed the Battalion. Croatan National Forest soon turned into a marshy swampland, the roads became drainage ditches and rivers enlarged into lakes, but the maneuvers were held as planned. It was a sort of amphibious warfare.

There were three problems, each of three days' duration, with a short rest and reorganization period between each. The men marched, sweated, deployed and redeployed, attacked and re-treated, built roads and roadblocks, and in short, performed their functions as Engineers in such a manner as to merit sincere congratulations and praise from Brigadier General Rollin A. Tilton, Commanding General of the Chesapeake Bay Sector. Few in Companies A and C and H&S Company will forget the crossing of a river, made in assault boats in the middle of the night, and the surprise attack and complete rout of the "enemy," soundly asleep on the other side; and the capture of Company B, which was the "enemy," and its kitchen truck.

At the end of the third problem the maneuvers were declared over, and a review of the entire Mobile Forces took place in the Regimental Bivouac Area, complete with color guard and band. Later, in camps in the States and in water-filled foxholes in the Pacific, the men laughed while reminiscing over the two weeks spent at Croatan. Those men in Lieutenant Mike Cassis' 3d Platoon, Company A, laughed especially heartily remembering the looks of surprise and bewilderment that came over the faces of the infantrymen on that eventful night of the river crossing, when with careless abandon, the men of the platoon tossed small blocks of nitro-starch and TNT under and around the sleeping men, next to their tents, under their trucks and in the air over their heads, doing no material damage, but causing hearts to skip a beat and giving added impetus to their already swiftly moving legs. Nor will anyone who participated forget the five-mile march to a demonstration area with the air shimmering as the temperature neared the one-hundred degree mark. The men dropped out along the way, one by one and then in pairs, faster than the medics could keep up with them. Infantrymen and Engineers alike were exhausted, sun-stricken, and too weary to go farther.

When the units of Mobile Force returned to their respective camps, the 233d remained for further training. The Battalion engaged in the repair of the roads and fences destroyed by the troops during maneuvers.

Private Gordon R. Tobin at this time was sent to Fort Belvoir, Virginia, to attend a course in water purification.

After the completion of this task the Battalion, bivouacking on the well remembered "nine-foot-road," engaged in technical engineer training including two weeks' training with engineer equipment of the Marine Corps, at Camp Lejeune, New River, North Carolina. While at Lejeune, the men marched by companies to the mock-up, a simulated transport made of wood, with nets over one side, and embarked in the small landing craft to hit the small strip of sandy beach. This operation would become all too familiar, in time.

WE TRAIN FOR THE BEACHES

The next phase of training was to instruct the men in the 233d's future profession; with advanced amphibious training they became proficient as Shore Party Engineers. Their future in the Pacific was sealed. On the 29th of August they left North Carolina, returning to their respective stations. During maneuvers, Lieutenant Roland D. Vandale took command of Company B; when Company A returned to Camp Somerset, Lieutenant John E. Crain succeeded Captain Eugene E. Skogerson, who was assigned to battalion headquarters. Another move was coming soon, this time a change of station.

On September 13, 1943, again in motor convoy, the Battalion set out for Camp Pickett, Virginia. The trip was uneventful, but upon arriving at Camp Pickett the men could hardly believe their eyes. Here was Utopia. Here were mess halls, big white two-story barracks, service clubs, theatres, paved streets and in short—civilization. But the convoy rolled on. Everyone strained to catch the first glimpse of "our barracks." The convoy rolled on. The paved streets were thinning out. The barracks weren't so numerous now. The service clubs had been passed ten minutes ago. The convoy rolled on. Still the pavement rumbled under the wheels. Soon the smooth ride became bumpy, dusty. Concrete roads gave way to dirt roads. Barracks were replaced by trees, and when the convoy did stop the men were greeted with a 10-acre patch of virgin pasture. And, there on the native sod by Birchin Lake, the battalion erected a tent city, complete with chimneys on every canvas roof.

The Battalion was attached to the 1118th Engineer Combat Group, consisting of a Headquarters and Headquarters Company and the 132d, 242d and 233d Engineer Combat Battalions. The entire group was assigned to the XIII Corps for final training.

Birchin Lake Area, about the size of the average city block, became the scene of much activity. The training schedule concentrated on building 25-ton ponton bridges, 300-foot infantry footbridges, and many other water-crossing structures and expedients. On Sundays the men went swimming. In the wooded areas around the camp they learned how to construct and tear down the heavy H-10 bridge and the prefabricated steel Bailey bridge, sometimes during the day, but usually at night. Speed marches and 25-mile hikes rounded out the training schedule, and the men of the Battalion were becoming proficient and sturdy. Muscles strengthened and became hard. Legs became accustomed to gruelling hours of marching and hiking over rough terrain. Engineering work became second nature and the Battalion was shaping into a top-grade weapon of war. Captain Clarence E. Johnson, Captain Nicholas C. Angel, and Captain Christian C. Lutz were in command of Companies A, H&S, and C, respectively. Captain Roland D. Vandale commanded Company B. At the completion of this phase of training, another move was ordered for the Battalion.

This was the first overland rail movement the Battalion made. Many problems of preparation were ironed out, and on October 15, 1943 the move to Fort Pierce, Florida, a United States Naval Amphibious Training Base of the Atlantic Fleet, was started. Here was to begin the final indoctrination of the 233d Engineers. Here they were to learn amphibious warfare, shore party engineering and beach organization. Here they were to become accustomed to ships and landing craft. The men were going to be sea-sick. They were going to get wet. They were going to prepare themselves for beaches in the Pacific, for the Jap, for real war. The long, hazardous road to Tokyo loomed ahead. Perhaps here the future destiny of the Battalion was decided, for it was at Fort Pierce that they became full-fledged combat engineers, well trained as shore-party engineers.

Upon arrival at the Fort they were met by a Navy band and escorted to the camp area, an island accessible only by a bridge. Pyramidal tents again, this time with wooden floors, screened in all around, with a screen door in front. Such luxuries couldn't last. Training began immediately. At this time, more men were sent to specialist's schools: Private Harold Proudfoot, to Water Purification School at Fort Belvoir, Virginia; and Privates Gerald J. Jahnke, Leonard W. Pitlyk, William H. Orr, Jr., and Elmer H. Dessert to Signal Communications School at Camp Crowder, Missouri.

For this training, Naval beach parties were attached to the Battalion, one to each line company and a smaller one to H&S Company. Trucks were waterproofed, their long rubber hoses set at crazy angles, and noisy exhaust extensions were added. Sergeant Graddie Woods, the Battalion Motor Sergeant, and the Company Motor Sergeants, Jones, Armstrong and Dicks, were learning the preparations they and their mechanics were going to be making on the Battalion's rolling stock time after time in the future.

The companies were no longer conventional organizations. Instead of Headquarters, 1st, 2d and 3d Platoons, they became Command Group, Ship's Platoon, Service Platoon, Liaison Section, MP Section, Engineering Section, etc. Each man was given a boat-team number, made up of the number of his respective boat's assault wave and boat number in that wave. For instance, when a call came for Boat Team 34, the men assigned to the third wave, fourth boat would scramble up the ladder of the mock-up, down a cargo net, and into their boat, waiting in the water below. When all the waves were formed and circling offshore, they would successively, in numbered waves, hit the beach. Priority equipment was hand-carried by the individual, and as soon as the beaches were organized, the supplies would begin to pour ashore.

For six weeks the men climbed over the mock-up, floated around in landing craft and came ashore on the Florida coastline. At completion of this training the Battalion returned to Camp Pickett, Virginia. The past training of the fast-learning men was going to become of use, for on November 24, 1943 the Battalion was alerted for another movement—overseas.

Arriving at Camp Pickett the men set up housekeeping again, still in the all-too-familiar pyramidal tents. The first three graders "enjoyed" a day of kitchen police on Thanksgiving, and a real feast marked the holiday. Rumor had it that these top-ranking sergeants were thankful, on that day of Thanksgiving, that kitchen police was not one of their assigned duties. Two weeks later, at Pickett, the Battalion moved uptown on Twenty-fourth Street. The men knew that they were really getting up in the world. Just look—they lived on a paved street and in barracks. Built of wood, too.

Another move was made on the 28th of December, 1943 to Solomons Island, Maryland, by motorized convoy. After the offensive tactics learned in Florida, the Battalion was now going to participate in maneuvers of a somewhat different type. This was to be a defensive practice against an attacking amphibious combat team of the 77th Infantry Division.

"Oh, well!" the men commented, "we might as well learn both sides of the question." They did. Simulated defensive positions were taken up along the beaches of the expected "attack," and four different phase lines were prepared to fall back to if conditions warranted. All command posts were connected by field telephone and radio so the various commanders could be kept informed of the changes in the situation. On New Year's Eve the Battalion, snugly freezing in its foxholes with temperature steadily dropping and snow falling all around, waited for the attack and listened to the strains of "Auld Lang Syne," coming softly from a radio in one of the command cars. The combat team by no means walked ashore with ease. Mission completed, the Battalion returned to Camp Pickett on the 3d of January, 1944.

On the 20th of January, 1944 they again departed, by train, for Norfolk, Virginia, to embark for training as shore-party engineers for the 307th Regimental Combat Team of the 77th Division. This was to be the final exam on the lessons these engineers had learned since the 12th of January, 1943 when the unit had been activated as the 233d Engineer Combat Battalion.

The companies were formed in accordance with shore engineer requirements. Everything was to be the same as at Fort Pierce, except that here the men would be using real transports instead of the mock-ups. It was the first taste the men had of life aboard a troop transport. Each company was with a different battalion of the 307th Infantry Regiment, Company A with the 1st Battalion, Company B with the 2d Battalion, and Company C with the 3d Battalion. Headquarters was with Regimental Headquarters and the remainder of H&S Company was split up among the other companies. Company A embarked on the APA (Attack Personnel Armored) 45, USS *Henrico*; Company B on the APA 26, USS *Chase*; Company C on the APA 38, USS *Chilton*; and Headquarters on the regimental flagship, APA 44, USS *Fremont*. All of the ships were brand-new, especially built for their special job; all were sister ships, having been built at the same time; and eighteen months later all had been damaged by the Japs in the waters of the Pacific: the *Henrico*, seriously; the *Fremont*, sunk.

The trip to the Solomons Island maneuver area lasted not quite a week, but during that time the men were thoroughly schooled in life aboard an APA. Embarkation and debarkation drills, fire drills, gas drills, defense against enemy attack were repeated until the men were secretly hoping for something actually to happen!

Without further event, however, D-day, H-hour arrived, the nets were thrown over the sides of the ships, boats were lowered into the water, and the 233d began its first full-scale amphibious operation. From that moment on, it was just like Florida. The ride to the beach in the landing craft, setting up the dumps, constructing roads inland and along the beach, setting up defensive positions against land, sea and air attacks, were all the same.

The big difference was the fact that the men had an audience, and quite a distinguished audience—high-ranking army and navy officers from several of the Allied Powers: China, France, England and Russia; Senators and Representatives; the then Secretary of the Navy, Mr. Frank Knox; and the then Under Secretary of War, Mr. Robert P. Patterson. The work progressed smoothly and the beaches and dumps were set up in record time. Although a heavy sea was running, not one landing craft foundered, and all cargo was transferred to the shore without loss. The combined efforts of nature made things difficult: rain and snow, heavy surf, and men almost freezing all proved far from being exhilarating— but aside from all of that was the invaluable experience gained.

Upon returning to Camp Pickett, physical training programs were stressed, orientation lectures became numerous, solid boxes and crates were built, and final equipment inspections were made to insure that every man and company had assigned equipment and that this equipment was in perfect condition. All during this period of preparedness replacements were constantly arriving from camps throughout the country. At the same time, all those men in the Battalion found to be physically unfit for overseas service, were transferred or discharged. The Battalion gradually assumed a size larger than its authorized strength, but as it was moving overseas, this was necessary. Just as final preparations were being completed, Lieutenant Colonel Clayton S. Gates, who had commanded the Battalion since its activation, died on the 4th of March, 1944 and Lieutenant Colonel Alexander W. Jurvic assumed command, with Major Orlan A. Johnson as executive officer. To honor Colonel Gates and to receive Colonel Jurvic, the Battalion held a review on the 6th of March, 1944 on the parade ground at Camp Pickett. Music was furnished by the 77th Division Band. The announcement by the Battalion adjutant, Lieutenant Thomas G. Blair, at the beginning of the ceremonies, "Colonel Gates is dead . . ." will never be forgotten by the men who were present. Those men knew they had lost a fine leader and friend.

On the 8th of March, 1944 the Battalion entrained for the Seattle Port of Embarkation at Seattle, Washington, and arrived at Fort Lawton, Washington, on the 12th of March. There the men were processed for their movement overseas, and last-minute supplies were issued. Shots, in what seemed dozen lots, were administered in the first few days. These were followed by more orientation lectures, war bond lectures, insurance lectures, movies, lectures and more lectures, until four days later when the men were finally given passes, they fairly staggered out of the gate. Seattle proved to be the best city that the men had been stationed near and the entire personnel of the organization took their one last fling. Monday night, the 20th of March, found the entire Battalion aboard the U. S. Army Transport *Noordam,* a converted Dutch passenger and freight vessel. It was soon the expressed opinion of the men living down in the holds that we should give it back to the Dutch.

Life aboard the *Noordam,* for a good many men, wasn't too pleasant. It was their first sea voyage. Troop spaces were crowded, as was rail space for the eighty per cent that were having their first taste of seasickness. Feeding was twice a day and a couple of hours in line each time. Blackout at night, and a swaying, rocking, rolling bed helped little to enhance the niceties of the voyage. Everyone sincerely hoped that this wasn't an example of all G.I. sea voyages. Spirits rose on the 28th of March, 1944 when land was sighted.

CHAPTER III

HAWAII

Grass-skirted, sepia-toned dancing girls did *not* meet us at the dock of Honolulu. The Army seemingly wants to slip these things to you gradually so we were welcomed by an Army band rendering "Aloha," quickly transferred to sugar-cane cars on the local railroad and shuttled off into the tropical night. It was a beautiful night, with occasional rain, and soon we were rattling and bumping along the coast toward the western side of the island of Oahu. We rolled on in this manner for hours. The men stood for most of the journey because Hawaiian rolling stock is minus springs. Well past midnight, after traversing two-thirds of the coast line of the 40-mile island, we arrived. Probably nothing has ever been as black as night in a cane field at 0200 on the morning of the 29th of March, 1944. Then came much waiting, a quick ride in a six-by-six and considerable stumbling around on a hillside. Then we found it, or at least our part of it: Camp Kahuku, Oahu, Territory of Hawaii.

Both the pyramidal tents and occasional five-minute downpours for which we had been prepared, were there. There were sandwiches and good hot coffee waiting. There were also cots and mosquitoes.

At 0600, reveille. On looking around, one found that the men's faces resembled the surrounding terrain. Here rose a bump, there a welt, and eyes peered out from under lumpy swollen eyelids. The famous Hawaiian mosquitoes had extended their greeting during the short three hours of sleep had by all except the cooks, who already had our chow coming up. And here was our new home, Camp Kahuku—one continuous hump after another. It started up the hillside, above the highest sugar-cane field, and extended as high as one could climb. It was located on the extreme northern end of the island, forty miles from Honolulu, and being on the west slope of the hills, it presented an ideal track for the wind, whistling around the northern slope, to continue its sweep. This it did for our entire stay at Kahuku. The address of the Battalion was now an APO number.

First, camp was put in order, access roads were rebuilt and

It started up the hillside, above the highest sugarcane field, and extended as high as one could climb.

widened, and the entire area in general was made as comfortable as possible. A week later the 307th Combat Team, 77th Infantry Division, arrived at Camp Kahuku. The 233d was assigned to the combat team as engineer shore party. The extensive training period that followed was to knit more firmly the various units that went to make up the team. All types of combat engineer work were reviewed: flamethrower tactics, assaults on fortified positions, beach defenses, etc. Most of the technicians attended schools for advance and refresher courses in their particular line of work. A class in scouting and patrolling was organized, the reconnaissance personnel of the companies and the Battalion Section attending. A very noticeable change took place in the medical detachment: they were going to fight Japs now. They needed weapons, and they got them. The motor pool began to swell in size. New and different types of equipment were added. Cranes, larger bulldozers, more trucks, light plants, water distillation units, and numerous other items began to appear.

Here also we accumulated some two hundred records for our public address system. Special Service radios were acquired and packed and complete assortments of athletic equipment were

Demolitions exploded underfoot and machine-gun fire grazed overhead.

issued to each company, but it was to be many, many months before we were to use what was left of these recreational items.

Our jungle packs began to take on size with the acquisition of necessary new items, and one would look back at those 25-mile marches in Virginia, glance at the now swelling load, and wonder. Yes, it was going to be all this and jungle too. We got jungle medical kits, three times the size of a Stateside first-aid kit, an extra canteen complete with cover and cup, bug powder, aerosol bombs, heating tablets, morphine syrettes, gas masks, gas capes and ointments, trench knives, compasses, extra magazines, and a host of other items that each man would have to carry. We felt, from the looks of the equipment coming in, that we were going to be well equipped. We hadn't heard of New Caledonia yet.

In order to become familiar with jungle tactics, the Battalion moved to the Unit Jungle Training Center, located on the east side of Oahu. Here the Center had duplicated jungle conditions. The courses were rough and rugged with caution seemingly thrown to the winds. Great emphasis was placed on physical hardening. Scratches, cuts, bruises and broken bones were commonplace. The classes were run on split-second timing with trucks to shuttle the men from class to class. A typical morning consisted of forty-five minutes of calisthenics, an hour of demolitions, an hour of stream-crossing techniques, an hour of barbed wire, and an hour on how to live in the jungle. The afternoon was much the same and at night there was an occasional problem to keep one sharp. The reaction courses were as near actual combat as man

The men learned to fire a caliber .30.

could conceive. These were barbed-wire infested courses, with the latest in mud holes, demolitions exploding underfoot, and machine-gun fire grazing overhead.

Captain Robert K. Graham (then Lieutenant) was in charge of one of the stream-crossing courses. His course consisted of learning every conceivable way to cross a stream with the least possible equipment. Rope bridges, brushwood boats, wooden footbridges floating on gasoline drums, rafts, and many more methods were demonstrated, built and tried out here. Lieutenants Max L. Daley and Romaine S. Foss conducted a course in barbed-wire entanglements and how to get through them, including the proper method to breach an entanglement with the bangalore torpedo. On the combat firing range the men learned to fire a .30-caliber machine gun from the hip. They learned to fire all small caliber weapons under jungle and combat conditions. In the jungle-living class they were taught what to eat in the jungle, how to build a suitable shelter with natural materials gathered in the jungle, how to locate drinking water, how to purify it, how to drink it without waste. Night problems were frequent, teaching the men the use of the compass in the jungle. Street fighting, bayonet courses, and house-to-house fighting rounded out the program. Every conceivable type of knowledge, gained by men who had actual experience in the Pacific, was taught here at Jungle Training to the men who needed to learn everything they could.

On the 3d of May, 1944 Lieutenant Colonel Jurvic was transferred to Headquarters, Pacific Ocean Areas, and Major Orlan A. Johnson assumed command of the Battalion.

Upon returning from Jungle Training to Camp Kahuku, in addition to the continued training the Battalion received a work order. There was construction to be done at Kahuku Army Air Base, under control of the Seventh Air Force. The 233d was one of the engineer battalions assigned to this work. Tent floors and frames, mess halls, washrooms, day rooms and supply buildings were built. Areas were leveled, coral was hauled to surface huge areas, and through all this the men of the battalion continued to prepare themselves for what was ahead, for beaches on islands to the west, and for combat.

One enjoyable part of this preparation was the swimming classes conducted by Lieutenant Henry A. Lind and the top swimmers of the Battalion. Every man in the Battalion was tested and required to display ability as a swimmer with and without clothes. Those men not qualifying were divided into classes, and on a small, beautiful sandy-shore beach in the vicinity of the town of Kahuku, they spent hours daily until all members of the Battalion were able to handle themselves efficiently in the water.

It wasn't all work and no play on Hawaii, however. Recreation facilities were excellent. Passes to Honolulu were frequent, and not hard to obtain. One of the most favored rendezvous of the men was not Honolulu, however—it was the USO Beach Club, in Kahuku. Here there were facilities for swimming, volley ball, lawn sports; there was a beautiful native cottage-by-the-sea converted to a clubhouse with snack bar, music rooms, ping-pong tables, and a writing room. In all, it was a place where the men could spend a Sunday afternoon enjoyably with surroundings reminiscent of the States and home.

Down the beach a short distance was another enjoyable spot. Here the officers of the Kahuku Army Air Base had established their Officers' Club. They generously extended an open-house invitation to the officers of the 233d. This privilege they accepted, spending many enjoyable hours with the officers of the Seventh Air Force stationed at the Kahuku Base.

The post exchange in camp left nothing to be desired. Beer was plentiful. There seemed to be a never-ending stream of men from the post exchange to their tents, carrying cases of golden brew. Music and news were supplied over the Battalion's public address system, "Station ENGR, Kahuku, where the wind blows freely, and the stars shine bright." The days were begun to the tune, "Sunny Side of the Street" and ended with "The Lord's Prayer" set to music.

As is customary in all regiments and separate battalions, the 233d had adopted a basic plan for a battalion insignia. It had been approved before the unit left the States, but would not be authorized until after the present war was over and a history of the unit's campaigns was depicted upon it. The insignia was in the shape of a shield of white bricks, with red mortar—this representing construction—and imposed across the brick wall was a huge scrawling griffin, the dragon of destruction—which represented demolition. At Kahuku the name "Griffins" and the caricature of a fiery-red dragon became the symbol of the 233d Engineers.

Under the direction and editorship of Captain Theodore C. Meinelt, assisted by Technical Sergeant Harvey J. Field, Sergeant Carl A. Senal and numerous other talented members of the Battalion, the first overseas printing of the Battalion Weekly was inaugurated. It was named "The Griffin," and until VJ-day this unit publication appeared weekly, conditions permitting. Here too, with this initial printing and the use of the word "Griffin," the 233d Engineers acquired the name of Griffins, a name that was still much in evidence in Kure, Honshu, Japan, in November, 1945 when the Griffins were sweating out their last move.

In the middle of June the Battalion participated in its last maneuver, a dry run at Waianae Beach, on Oahu, where the entire 307th Regimental Combat Team had its final combined amphibious training problem, taking cognizance of the latest methods learned in the previous operations in the Pacific. Here, the training period was completed for the Battalion—that is, the *pretraining* period, for a soldier never finishes his training. It became SOP after every action, job or operation in the future to continue to train the men at every possible opportunity in the latest methods, new weapons, and equipment, and from lessons learned by experience.

On the Battalion's return to Kahuku, final preparations monopolized the days and nights. The motor-pool sergeants exercised the knowledge gained in Florida, and they, with their mechanics, worked around the clock waterproofing vehicles and equipment that were to accompany the Battalion on the "Operation." All other equipment, supplies and vehicles were stowed in a storage area to be shipped with the Division's rear echelon to New Caledonia, the garden spot of the Pacific. Well, that's what people say who have been to New Caledonia. Feverish activity filled the coming two weeks and the air was charged with excitement. Where? When? Everyone was curious.

The Battalion's Transport Quartermaster Team, Lieutenant Victor E. Weaver, Lieutenant Carl C. Cook, Technical Sergeant Merrill Blackman, and Technician Fifth Grade Floyd K. Oglesby, was assigned to the 307th Combat Team TQM Section for the move. On the 1st of July, 1944 they went to Honolulu to plan and supervise the loading of the SS *China Victory*, a Merchant Marine vessel assigned to carry supplies for thirty days and a number of vehicles for the combat team. The Battalion was well represented in the 100-man working parties sent down to accomplish this loading, working in 12-hour shifts. The TQM Team—this was their first experience in ship loading—soon learned that loading a ship for combat was not merely a pastime.

On the 7th of July, 1944, the Division was loaded, and the soft moonlit nights of Hawaii, the wind blowing around the peak at Kahuku, the souvenir-lined streets of Honolulu, Waikiki Beach, Pali Pass, Diamond Head—all were soon to fade into the past, and to remain as only a memory to the men of the 233d Engineers, for they were not destined to turn back on their "One-Way Road to Tokyo."

CHAPTER IV

WE GO TO WAR

On the morning of the 9th of July, 1944, a convoy quietly slipped from Honolulu Harbor, bound for Guam. Aboard the various ships, along with other troops, rode the 233d Engineers. Since the 25th of January, 1943 the date this unit was designated an Engineer Combat Battalion, these engineers had trained for combat. Now the 233d was going to war.

The USS *Monrovia*, flagship of the 307th Combat Team, led the center right column of the formation. Major Orlan A. Johnson, commanding officer of the 233d, with his staff and headquarters personnel, was aboard. He was new in his command, new to his troops, but he had great confidence in them. For the past few weeks he had watched the Battalion in its final training. Lieutenant Colonel Clayton S. Gates had trained them well.

In the wake of the *Monrovia* steamed the USS *Alcione*, carrying the 1st Battalion, 307th Infantry, and Company A, 233d Engineers, commanded by Captain Clarence E. Johnson. Captain Johnson knew his men and he was known to most of them as Dizz Johnson, a fact he was not aware of at the time. He knew they were well trained, and the job ahead, whatever it might be, presented no fears to Company A. Dizz knew they could do it.

To the rear of the *Alcione* followed the USS *Funston* carrying the 2d Battalion, 307th Infantry, and Company B, 233d Engineers. Captain Roland D. Vandale commanded Company B. He too had a definite feeling of confidence in his company. The jobs didn't come too big or too rugged for Company B. Company B was just as rugged as the job could be.

Next in the column was the USS *War Hawk* carrying the 3d Battalion, 307th Infantry, and Company C, 233d Engineers, commanded by Captain Christian C. Lutz. Captain Lutz, a veteran of Pearl Harbor, had a score to settle. His company was a well-trained, smooth-working machine, and the men of Company C, like their leader, held only one thought of any job: we can do it.

Scattered throughout the four ships was Headquarters and Service Company, 233d Engineers, commanded by Captain Nicholas C. Angel. His company, unlike the line companies, was divided between the headquarters detachment and those three line

These Engineers had trained for combat.

companies, and Nick, as he soon became known to everybody, seemingly rode alone. But where the men of H&S Company went Nick went also, for he had a profound affection for his men. They were all well trained specialists. Their duties were specific. Their training had been exacting, strenuous and complete. There were Cater, Field, Blackman, Muratore, Carol, Taylor, Becker, Woods, Flanders and many more, all important in the functioning of the Battalion. They would do their job and do it well. Nick had no fear that they wouldn't, although he would have liked to be with them these last few hours.

So there you have it. The 233d going to war. Five commanders, each in his own right, full of confidence. A Battalion made up of four companies, divided to their respective assignments, united in a common goal. "Whatever the job, we can do it." In the months that followed, that feeling of "can do" was to become a tradition, was to climax each achievement, because there was always another job to be done.

Uneventful days followed, and much time was devoted to planning. Maps appeared. Beach conditions were studied. Coral reefs became a topic of much conversation. When the men looked at maps of the Guam shoreline, their thoughts naturally turned to the hope that the stretch of beach with the narrowest coral reef would be chosen for the landings. All the beaches used in training had been sandy, but the men were well acquainted with sharp jagged underwater coral. Their feet had made contact, on many occasions, with coral reefs while they were swimming along the coast

Clearly defined were the beaches selected for the Guam invasion.

of Oahu. They preferred a sandy beach to work on, but to their dismay, Guam was going to be coral. Clearly defined on the maps were the beaches selected for the Guam invasion, and coral was much in evidence, for the reefs jutted out from the shoreline on these selected beaches from 200 to 500 yards.

It was during these first few days of the voyage that the men became familiar with: "Now hear this!" drawled over the ship's loudspeaker.

They learned where and when they would abandon ship should the worst happen; what to do during General Quarters, should the enemy attack; when chow was served and where; and the best way to descend or ascend a cargo net. Training and orientation were continued. The "sack," a piece of canvas swinging in a pipe frame, was welcome when night came. On the morning of the ninth day land was sighted.

"Now hear this! The land directly to our bow is the atoll of Eniwetok, in the Marshall Group." The sterns of the ships rose slightly as everyone rushed to the bow to get a look at land again.

Eniwetok consists of a group of islands forming a great circle. The water thus inclosed forms a safe anchorage, and soon the entire convoy lay at anchor within the circle. Food and water, fuel and last-minute supplies came over the side. Mail, flown out from Hawaii, was distributed. That night all hands were treated to a movie on deck. By daylight the next morning we were underway, with Guam four days ahead of us.

The problems of unloading became all-important now. To the shore-party commander fell the responsibility of directing the unloading on the beach, and to the shore-party engineers the entire job of unloading. This was going to be our part of the show. We were going to put the supplies and equipment of the 307th Combat Team on Guam.

One platoon (forty-two men) from each company was designated as a ship's platoon, and while ship's personnel would operate the booms and the landing craft, the job of handling the cargo and vehicles in the holds and in the landing craft alongside the ships was solely that of the ship's platoon. Thus Lieutenant Charles E. Schaub, of A Company; Lieutenant Peter J. Langhans, of B Company; and Lieutenant Henry A. Lind, of C Company, were to operate their platoons on their respective ships. During the last four days these four platoon leaders with their platoon sergeants spent endless hours organizing working details, planning their operations according to the TQM's plan, and sweating out the moment when the first vehicle or netload of cargo would go over the side. Then there could be no mistakes. The unloading, from the first lift until the last, must go as planned. The troops ashore depended on these ship's platoons for artillery, ammunition, gas, trucks, guns, rations, water and medical supplies. The work must proceed smoothly, with speed.

"There is a change of plans. The General wants tanks!"

"Can you move that wrecker to the side and get that ambulance out first?"

"Get twenty men on these guylines. Watch her when she clears the coaming! Take up slack on the starboard. Do it now!"

"Lower away!"

"Not Ten-in-one, Sergeant; they want K and C."

"I wonder how it's going in there. They keep calling for 105s more tanks—going must be tough."

"Heave to, men! All hands! Let's give 'em the stuff!"

There could be no mistakes, their work must proceed smoothly and speedily.

During these four preceding days there was another group of busy soldiers. These were the men known as Transport Quartermasters, usually called TQMs. Theirs was the job of loading and unloading the ships. The Battalion's TQMs aboard the *China Victory* were new at this job. None of the four men was an experienced stevedore. The largest conveyance any of them had loaded before was the turtleback of a Model A Ford coupe. This time they had loaded the *China Victory* with thirty-four hundred tons of vehicles and cargo. Aboard her they had stowed sixty medium tanks, thirty-six light tanks, trucks and jeeps totaling 139 vehicles, thirty days of supplies for the Combat Team, including gas and oil, and rations by the hundreds of cases, 650 tons of ammunition, nineteen outboard motors, fifty-four 10-man rubber boats, lumber, wire, T.N.T., clothing, shoes, mosquito repellent, salt tablets, arms, bandages, typewriter ribbons, and thousands of other needed items. Their load was a floating warehouse, and each item was important, necessary to the successful completion of the Combat Team's mission.

Technician Fifth Grade Floyd K. Oglesby kept the records of the load. He knew which small corner of the huge freighter held fragmentation grenades. He knew how many drums of eighty-octane gas were aboard, where small-arms repair trucks were stowed, how many vehicles would have to be moved to get a searchlight out. When something was unloaded he recorded it. He could tell you how much of anything was left aboard all through the unloading. In the early stages of his battle of Guam, Oglesby's weapons were pencils and his ammunition was figures.

Technical Sergeant Merrill Blackman supervised the unloading operations. He directed the working parties of the ship's platoon, improvised ways to do the impossible and to get into the landing craft those items needed ashore *when* they were needed ashore.

During the first day of the 77th Division's participation in the Guam Operation, Blacky, as Sergeant Blackman was called, received as his first message from the beach the following:

"Imperative we have all 10-man rubber boats ashore at once to get the wounded over reef to hospital ship. How many can you unload at once? When can you unload all? Advise." Blackman turned to Oglesby with the message and asked, "How many do we have?"

"Fifty-four aboard," Oglesby consulted his records. "Ten in hold three, upper-tween deck, right on top. The rest in hold of hold section three against the skin on the port side. They are behind all of those tanks and under two decks of cargo."

Blacky listened, then he answered the message, "Ten at once. Forty-four within two hours. Total fifty-four."

Oglesby glanced up at this tall gangling sergeant, after reading the message, and wondered how he was going to get forty-four cased rubber boats out of the bottom of a hold under two decks of cargo. Those cases weighed six hundred pounds apiece! He shrugged his shoulders and rushed off to the radio shack topside to dispatch the message, leaving Blacky to figure it out. But Blacky was not thinking, "Can I get them out?" He was figuring, "How can I get them out?"

There was a ladder well alongside of each hold section running to the bottom of each hold. There were doors leading into each deck. It was a small passageway, but maybe it would work. Blacky measured the doors, the diameter of the ladder well, the hatch openings in the well between decks, and found that his smallest opening was slightly less than three feet square. By knocking the crates off he could somehow squeeze these deflated rubber boats through the openings if he could get them over to the door. He ordered ten men of the ship's platoon to open Number Three and get the ten boats in there over the side. The landing craft were already coming alongside of Number Three. He took the rest of the platoon down to the bottom of Hold Three, and proceeded to make good on his message. For under the direction of Sergeant Blackman the men unpacked the boats, dragged them, one at a time, over the tanks and under a truck which was parked right at the entrance to the door, and forced them through the door into the bottom of the ladder well. Here a line was tied around them, and a group of the men who had gone topside started the long pull up to the deck. As these 600-pound rolls of rubber came to the hatch openings between the decks, more men climbed under them and pushed and shoved and kicked until they were through and then followed them up to the next opening where they repeated the pushing, shoving and kicking. Men sweated and swore, heaved and tugged, blistered their hands, knocked the skin from their knuckles, but rubber boats kept coming out of the hold, over the side of the ship to the waiting landing craft where they were rushed to the edge of the coral reef.

Here other engineers inflated them, floated them across the 200-yard reef to the beach, where still more engineers loaded wounded soldiers into them, and wading along side, floated them back out across the treacherous reef through the surf to waiting landing craft that took the wounded speedily to the hospital ship.

"Ten at once." That was easy. They were right on top of the load.

"Forty-four within two hours." That was impossible. They were on the bottom of the loaded ship, but Sergeant Merrill Blackman tackled the task with "can do."

Yes, as the convoy sped towards Guam and the coming operation, the men assigned TQM jobs were going to be busy soldiers.

About 2400, on the 21st of July, 1944 men on deck could see a red glow in the sky off the starboard bow. There it was in all its reality, what they had been training for, what they had read about and heard about. War! What was it going to be like?

CHAPTER V

WE MEET THE ENEMY

The initial landings on Guam were to be made by the Marines. Army troops were to be held in floating reserve and to go ashore only if needed. They were needed. When our convoy arrived in the transport area off the village of Agat on the west side of the island just south of the Orote Peninsula, at 0400 on the 22d of July, 1944 the Marines had been ashore since 0800 the morning before. The cruisers, battleships, and destroyers, lying offshore, were pouring tons of shells onto the island. The rumble of the big guns was like a continued roar of thunder. Flashes from shell bursts were everywhere on the visible part of the island. Star-shell flares lighted parts of the island like day. The men of the Army watched from their ships. The 77th Division and attached troops, including the 233d, were getting their first look-see at real war. Soon they would be a part of it.

By daylight liaison parties were on the way ashore. They landed on the already established Marine beaches. A boat loaded with officers from each infantry battalion was going ashore to look the situation over. They would formulate plans as to where, when and how the Division would be landed. The company commanders of the combat engineer battalions, the shore-party commanders, were a part of these liaison parties. They were destined to play a big part in the activities of the next few days.

According to plan the 77th Division Headquarters landed on the beach at Agat on the 24th of July, 1944 and a provisional Division shore party was organized. Lieutenant Colonel Newcomb, commanding officer of the 242d Engineer Combat Battalion, was appointed Divisional shore-party commander with the staff of the 233d Engineer Combat Battalion as his shore party staff. Major Orlan A. Johnson, commander of the 233d, was appointed executive officer. The remainder of the battalion then landed, wading ashore across the coral reef for a distance of almost three hundred yards. This was the most treacherous reef yet encountered in the Pacific War.

The entire Division was to be unloaded over White Beaches One and Two. Company A of the 233d was assigned general engineering duties; Company B was assigned to assist the 242d Engineer

Crates piled as high as the small cranes could reach.

Combat Battalion in the operation of White Beach Two; Company C was assigned to assist the 132d Engineer Combat Battalion in the operation of White Beach One and H&S Company was given the mission of defending the battalion area, about two hundred yards to the rear of White Beach Two.

Enemy contact with shore parties was negligible save for occasional sniper fire. There were no casualties in the Battalion due to enemy action. All the Divisional equipment, and supplies for thirty days for twenty thousand men, had to be dragged and carried over the reef. On any landing operation the unloading phase is a nightmare of aching backs—box upon box, oil drums, boats, boats and more boats loaded to the gunwales. This one was no exception for in addition to everything one could normally expect, there, almost blocking the entire beach, was the shell-pocked, water-covered reef stretching far out into the bay and extending the surf over hundreds of yards. The landing craft could come only to the edge of the reef and the engineers had to bridge the gap from the landing craft to the beach.

Cargo was unloaded from landing craft to amtrack and DUKW, from DUKW and amtrack to beach dump, from beach dump to truck and from truck to inland dump, where the supplies were issued or sent up front. Tons and tons of ammunition, oil, rations, gasoline, medical supplies and water were handled until every back

Gas drums were rolled into a swamp.

was breaking. Dozers, chains, mud, heavy surf, rising and receding tide, sand, ropes, stalled vehicles—and still the boats came to be unloaded. Vehicles were stalling all over the ocean-covered reef, unable to proceed ashore on their own drowned-out power. Here a jeep would run afoul of a water-covered shell-hole and drop out of sight, the driver swimming to shallow water, and over there was a tank with only its turret showing above the water. Boxes were piled as high as the small cranes could reach. Our big cranes didn't come along—no shipping space for them. Gas drums were rolled into a swamp. Everybody crossed and recrossed each other's path, getting in each other's way. This was chaos to the casual watcher, but the supplies kept coming ashore. Load after load was miraculously unloaded in the proper dump. More ammunition moved to the beach to resupply the initial units carried ashore by the troops up front. Wounded have to have medical supplies; soldiers need food and water—these things all had to be made available over that treacherous coral reef. The shore party engineers, at the end of hour after hour of sweat-producing, back-breaking labor would again hear the order, "Get those boats unloaded and that stuff ashore!"

"Unless the water was purified and treated."

They would glance up, smile, and bend their weary backs to the task. They were never finished. It was always another case of shells, a box of rations; they were beating the enemy by keeping the supplies rolling up to the front. And those smiles in answer to the order spoke always the same two words, "Can Do."

Night came. Sergeant Robert F. Cater and his electricians had the beach lights installed and the generator operating. They worked right on through the night, and the loaded landing craft still sloshed in to the edge of the reef. This would not cease until every box and carton on those loaded ships were ashore. To the shore party engineers, this was their battle of Guam.

During the day the motor pool, directed by Lieutenant Kondo W. Ruesch, had restarted and repaired an unknown number of stalled and disabled vehicles. Every vehicle we had was needed and must be kept running, for shipping space limitations had forced us to leave most of our trucks behind. The Battalion had landed on this operation with a total of twelve cargo and dump trucks, four per line company, instead of the twelve to fifteen each company was authorized. Like many other needed items, the remainder of our trucks had been shipped, with our rear echelon, to New Caledonia to await our arrival there.

Technical Sergeant Harvey J. Field had kept his map of the beach and surrounding occupied areas constantly up to date. Anyone coming ashore needed only to look at these maps to find which direction to go to find his headquarters or where his unit had set up.

Technical Sergeant David H. Flanders and his reconnaissance boys had worked hand in hand with Sergeant Field's section in keeping the maps posted. Throughout the day they had journeyed inland toward the front lines, dodging enemy fire, sloshing through knee-deep mud, crawling through underbrush and finding out where every unit had located. With the information gathered they reported back to Sergeant Field at the S-2 section. The draftsmen in Field's section then recorded the information on the maps. It was a directory service for the many soldiers coming ashore on an unknown island battleground.

Chief Warrant Officer George Lucas, over in Battalion Supply, Technical Sergeant Clarence L. Carroll, and the men in the S-4 section were looking after the food that would be needed by the men in the Battalion, and Captain Robert K. Graham, the Battalion Supply Officer, was locating gas and oil for the Battalion's equipment and directing the installation of a water point. Staff Sergeant Charlie Williams and the men in the water-supply section were installing the water point. Before the water was used Captain Graham had sent a squad of men up the stream to remove corpses of Japanese soldiers that had been killed in the action along the banks. Soldiers had to have water and the canned supply of water brought along wouldn't last very long. To drink from streams and springs meant dysentery unless the water was treated and purified. Another job for the combat engineers. On another section of the beach Technician Third Grade Bernice W. Vest and the men of the Battalion's medical detachment were busy in a quickly improvised aid station. Men who were hurt or wounded needed treatment and now these aid men were busy. Rest to them was something one merely talks about.

There was no sleep that first night. If an engineer wasn't working on the beaches he was manning a machine gun on the beachhead perimeter for protection against night-attacking Japs, or lying in his foxhole, gun in hand, listening for sounds between the patter of the raindrops, getting acquainted with scorpions, sand crabs and centipedes, or distinguishing between the usual night noises and the sounds of a creeping Jap soldier.

Thus the operation on the beaches went along, progressing rapidly throughout the first day and night and until 1800 on the second day, the 26th of July. Then a message of warning came to the shore party headquarters . . .

"Possible enemy counterattack from seaward. Prepare to defend the beaches against all intruders." We had heard about the night attacks from the sea on the Saipan beaches. The men had been especially trained for such an occasion. We could handle it if it came, but it could be costly and was certain to be a bloody affair. By 2300 that night the beaches were secured and all work had ceased. A complete defense had been set up to cover every foot of the beaches. Men waited in their foxholes, watching, their rifles loaded and their trench knives unsheathed and sticking in the bottom of their muddy foxholes, ready for use. A piece of driftwood, floating offshore, might look like a landing boat against the dim horizon. A thousand eyes would watch it as the men silently stared into the hazy darkness of the night.

The Japanese forces were still in possession of the end of the peninsula, and they were soon to make that fact well known. One of their 40mm dual-purpose automatic guns, far out on the peninsula, opened up on the beaches. White tracers arched for the White Beach area. Shells were falling thick on the beach. The Company C area was receiving most of it. From the beach, no one returned the fire. It was too far to the Jap gun position for our "fifties" to reach. The firing continued; men dug deeper into the slimy bottoms of their holes; minutes dragged into half an hour. The lucky ones on the beach watched the Company C area, wondering how soon the fire would shift and start falling in their own foxholes.

Out in the transport area, the men aboard the ships watched the white tracers race in an arc for White One and Two beach areas.

"Must be plenty tough in there tonight," said one fellow to his buddy.

"Yes, but look," came the answer. The second speaker pointed toward the ocean end of the peninsula. A sleek dark form slipped easily along the coast line of the peninsula about six hundred yards offshore. It was an American destroyer. The tracers from the Jap position continued to pour onto the beaches. Perhaps the

Jap gunner failed to see the trouble that was silently moving toward him. When the dark form was directly abreast of the menacing gun position it ceased to move. It became just another dark hull, like the many already standing off in the bay, but it was so very much closer to the Jap-held peninsula than the others.

"Baaalooom!!" The destroyer was outlined in a mass of flame for a short second; then the shells flashed as they exploded on the shore. The crack of the exploding missiles drifted out to sea, and minutes later, the men watching from those transports heard the sound. They cheered as it became evident that the tracers had ceased racing toward the beaches. Company C could rest a little easier and take a deep breath of gratitude for their team mates, the men in the U. S. Navy. It takes all services working together, to win a war and the men and officers of the 233d were fast learning this. Although he had caused no casualties in the ranks of the 233d, the Jap was giving them their first taste of combat, their baptism of fire.

CHAPTER VI

WE BUILD A ROAD

Lieutenant Colonel Orlan A. Johnson, then Major, was assigned the command of the Division Shore Party, vice Lieutenant Colonel Newcomb, on the 31st of July, 1944. By then, the Division had cut the island of Guam in half and was fast sweeping north, alongside the Marines, disposing of any enemy they met. A fast move such as this means longer supply lines. Roads became all-important now. The Division supply dumps had moved inland. They located about two miles north, along the Agat–Agaña road, and two miles to the east at the head of a valley on moderately high ground. A road had to be constructed from the Agat–Agaña Road, inland across the flat bottom of the valley, to these new dumps. Company A was assigned to the 302d Engineer Combat Battalion, division engineers for the 77th, and given the mission of constructing this access road.

The company moved to a spot near the junction of this new road, which became known as Johnson Road (or the 233d's Nightmare) and the Agat–Agaña Road. Perhaps it was named after First Sergeant Jack D. Johnson, of H&S Company; or Captain Clarence E. Johnson, the Company A commander; or Technician Fifth Grade Wallace M. Johnson, of the Medical Detachment or after the Battalion Commander, Orlan A. Johnson. But regardless of which Johnson it was named after, it became Johnson Road. And on Johnson Road every man of the Battalion, at some time or another, was introduced to the engineer's favorite weapon, the "idiot stick," and initiated in its use. An idiot stick, for the benefit of those who are not engineers, is a wooden handle upon one end of which is a metal beaker-like attachment. In using this weapon the engineer places the metal end in a mud hole and attempts to remove it—the mud hole. The Quartermaster calls the tool the shovel, pony, D-2.

From this junction, which was atop a small hill, the road sloped gently eastward towards the valley's bottom, then wound in and around the creek and marshes to the other side of the flats and turned north up the valley to the dumps. Here, Captain Clarence E. Johnson, with the assistance of Lieutenants George W. Gray, Max L. Daley, Charles E. Schaub and Carl C. Cook, his platoon

The bivouac was on high ground across to the east side of the valley.

commanders, and the NCOs and men of Company A, started the road. They spaded out a roadbed, borrowed a power shovel from the Seabees, and the coral began to roll. Johnson Road was taking shape. Right among the working parties, building the road, the supply traffic started to move the endless chain of supplies to the inland dumps.

On the beach two men from Company C were slightly wounded. On the 3d of August, 1944 Companies B and C were relieved from assisting the 132d and 242d Engineers, and were assigned as Shore Party Engineers at Dadi Beach, to assist the Marine Shore Party in its operation and to unload the remainder of the Division supplies. During the afternoon a group of natives, men and boys, came from the south in the vicinity of the town of Ematac, having escaped from the Japanese early that morning, and wanted to help the Americans fight. They were led into the bivouac area of the Battalion where they were fed and then taken to the Medical Detachment of the Battalion. Here, Captain Julius J. Simon and his aid men treated them, taking care of the various injuries caused by the terrain on their cross country trip. They were then turned over to Division officials.

The following morning H&S Company and Battalion Headquarters moved to the vicinity of the Division's inland dumps at the head of the still-progressing Johnson Road. Captain Richard S. Stevick, the Battalion Operations Officer, and his assistant, Lieutenant Otto W. Mourek, of Cicero, Illinois, were left on the beach in charge of all operations there. The bivouac was on high ground to the east side of the valley where Johnson Road turned north to the dump area. The landing of supplies continued on Dadi Beach, and the continuous string of trucks kept moving over Johnson Road to the dumps, while men working in and around the traffic continued to keep the almost impassable trail open, and improved the road. They gave their best to construct a road before the incessant rains made it completely impassable. That night men from Company A encountered a Japanese patrol on their perimeter, killing one Jap and dispersing the remainder.

Although on the 10th of August the island of Guam was declared secure, work progressed as usual on a 24-hour basis. For the 233d "work on a 24-hour basis" was then, and for the duration, a Battalion SOP. Companies B and C were relieved from their assignments as Shore Party on Dadi Beach and the entire Battalion, less Company A (still bivouacked at the entrance to Johnson Road), moved up to the location of H&S Company and Battalion Headquarters.

The Battalion radio operators had been temporarily assigned to the Joint Assault Signal Company for the operation. They had worked as shore fire-control teams, attached to the various battalions of the 77th Infantry Division. These teams transmitted fire-control messages from ground observers with the front-line troops to ships standing off the coast, to bring naval gunfire to bear on targets designated. Very often these men, carrying their radios on their backs, were in advance of the front-line troops. These radio operators—Technician Fourth Grade Carl L. Bath from the Reconnaissance Section of the Battalion; Technicians Fourth Grade Douglas A. Kohl, William E. Noack and William C. Friday from the Battalion Communications Section; Technicians Fourth Grade Sheldon J. Shalett and Gerald J. Jahnke from Company A; Technicians Fourth Grade John A. Bickford and Leonard W. Pitlyk; Technician Fifth Grade Stephen E. Hoffman from Company B, and Technicians Fifth Grade William H. Orr Jr., Earl J. Sanders and Elmer H. Dessert from Company C—separated from their own units and working with a strange group of men and officers, had attacked their job with that same "can do" attitude and produced results. They had done their job well, and they were commended very highly by the commanding officer of the Joint Assault Signal Company. Just another time when 233d Engineers had faced a hard job under the most trying conditions with their ever-present attitude of doing the job well at any cost.

This attitude—the will to do the job well—was never to die among the men of the Battalion, and soon it was demonstrated again in a most superior manner by the Medical Detachment. With the return of JASCO (Joint Assault Signal Company) from the front lines these radio operators returned to their own companies of the 233d, and JASCO set up its bivouac in an area adjacent to H&S Company. Captain Nicholas C. Angel sent his carpenters over to the JASCO to construct a screened-in kitchen. These men of JASCO had all undergone the exhausting exposure of the front lines—rain, mud, sleepless nights, mosquitoes and contaminated water. Dysentery was running high. Dengue fever caused by the daylight mosquitoes was taking its toll. In addition to the high sickness rate in the Battalion that was keeping the medics busy day and night, Captain Julius J. Simon, the Battalion Surgeon, generously accepted the sick from JASCO. His small aid station rapidly grew into an improvised hospital. With the strenuous sanitation measures demanded by the Battalion commander dysentery was kept to a minimum, but there was no apparent preventive measures against dengue fever except to keep from getting bitten by the daylight mosquito—a feat that was practically impossible.

Every available tent and the few cots smuggled along in bedrolls were turned over to the medics. Technician Third Grade Bernice W. Vest with his fourteen aid men assisted Captain Simon and went on a 24-hour basis along with the rest of the Battalion, for the continuous rains had by now turned the bed of Johnson Road into a huge lake of mud too thin for wheeled traffic to move in and too thick for DUKWs to float in. The supply of the proper kind of food and fruit juices was practically impossible, for the Army troops on Guam, long since supposed to be on their way to New Caledonia, had no source of supply after the initial 30-day supply was exhausted except through the Marines, whose supply was supposedly sufficient only for their own forces. Thus Captain Simon and his medical aid men ministered to the sick, with numbers now in the epidemic stages. For his devotion to the welfare of the men and officers of his Battalion as well as those of JASCO during this period, and for his ingenuity in improvising hospital care for these many patients with the supplies and equipment allotted to an aid station, Captain Julius J. Simon of New York City was awarded the Bronze Star Medal.

The incessant rains were not helping Johnson Road. The construction of the road at first had proceeded very fast. Now, with very few trucks to haul coral to top the road, and only a dozer or so for spreading the coral and pulling out the supply trucks that continually got stuck, Captain Johnson found the rains getting the better of the job. Company A had succeeded through

The men of Company A began to haul logs and place them in the marsh.

sheer persistence in surfacing the road for over a mile, which led them down the slope to the edge of the flat bottomless stretch the men soon named "the marsh." It was not a marsh in the usual sense but a low stretch of land crossed by a creek which drained the surrounding hills. Here was mud, bottomless, with only an occasional hassock or mound of dry soil. At first the drivers of the supply trucks had driven almost straight across the bottom, but as the continuous traffic turned the trail into a quagmire, the drivers moved the road to the south to seemingly firmer ground. Finally the entire area became one large area of deep soft ruts and mud that was impassable.

During this period Company A continued to haul coral and top the road foot by foot. It was an impossible task but the road had to be kept open. Dozers would pull loaded trucks the entire distance across the flats, and some days when the rain would cease for a spell the high places would dry out and support traffic. Finally the road reached a point where coral would no longer hold. There just wasn't any bottom to it at all. This is when an engineer turns to corduroy—logs to give flotation. But the coconut groves were far distant. Regardless, the men of Company A began to haul logs and place them in the marsh. It took six hundred logs in all before they had finally bridged the marsh.

On the other side Lieutenants Langhans, Lassetter, Hude and Hanson, and the men from Company B had started working on the road, bringing coral from a hill south of the Battalion area. Lieutenants Blair, Lind, Crawford and Petre and the men of Company C were working on the section of road running north from the

Patrols traversed areas that had not yet been covered by the infantry.

Battalion area to the dumps. A road was also constructed south from Johnson around the crest of the hill to the water point. Later this stretch of road built by Company C was to be the only means of getting food to the entire Division.

In addition to working on the road the dozers continued to pull ration and supply trucks through the unbuilt part of the route. In this manner traffic moved steadily over the road. Men not only worked 12-hour shifts but also around the clock, building a road through an impassable marshland, dozing trucks through the mud. This kept the supplies rolling up to the Division at the front and around to Harmon Road and Camp McNair after the Division had moved back. More than once H&S Company was called out to help drain the water from the road. It was like emptying a bathtub with an eye-dropper to dig a drainage ditch along a ribbon of mud with entrenching tools, but these were all that were available for the cooks, typists and clerks of H&S Company to work with.

Things soon would have been fine had the rains given us half a chance. No sooner was the Johnson Road completed across the marsh to the Battalion area with the help of six hundred logs, than its route was changed and now ran through the Battalion area and along the crest of the hill and down into the dump area. Then the rear echelon elements moved out to the Division area at Camp McNair and the dumps moved back to Dadi Beach. It now looked

Johnson Road was completed.

as if Johnson Road was to become a private road used only by the Battalion, JASCO and the 36th Field Hospital, which had just moved in below the Battalion on the now-completed road. This would be fine, thought the men, because even with only idiot sticks as our major weapon we could keep the road open. Johnson Road was ready.

The 233d had come a long way in the past few weeks. They had made their first real amphibious landing, met the enemy and weathered the normal hardships of any campaign—but better still they had found what the 233d could accomplish. Here their contact with the actual enemy had been negligible in comparison to that of the infantry foot soldier who met him face to face, but conquering the treacherous coral reef, the beach operations, and the complete subjugation of torrential rains, bottomless mud, lack of necessary equipment, and unobtainable supplies in construction of Johnson Road had bolstered their confidence. Whatever the job might be the 233d Combat Engineers could do it.

Further to train the men and to help with the mop-up of Guam the platoons of the various companies conducted two-day patrols over Mount Alaphan south to Facpi Point and return. These patrols traversed areas that had not yet been covered by the infantry. Though a total of nine patrols went into this enemy-inhabited country from the Battalion, no casualties were suffered due to enemy action. The luck that was to become a tradition with the Battalion was beginning to show up.

CHAPTER VII

C, K, AND TEN-IN-ONE

The 36th Field Hospital, moving in just below the Battalion Area, was a boon to Captain Simon and his detachment of aid men. The bed cases could be moved to the hospital and our medics could get some sleep. Even Major Johnson could now get his cot back.

Traffic was continuing as heavy as usual on Johnson Road and the motor pools were greatly over-burdened, since the few over-worked vehicles we had needed unobtainable parts. It was here that Lieutenant Rondo W. Ruesch and his mechanics discovered that the rear end of a DUKW, damaged beyond repair, could be welded in place of the rear end of a six-by-six $2\frac{1}{2}$-ton truck and made to work. Here, also, a jeep was constructed out of salvaged parts.

Truck drivers, too, were having their troubles. The men of the Battalion had to eat even though they were existing on field rations. Someone had to haul the rations, water, and fuel for the equipment. Privates First Class Floyd L. Bullard and Robert H. Klein were becoming mud drivers of the highest order. Mud to them was a challenge and they apparently delighted in defeating it, as did all the other Battalion drivers. Among them was a lad from Michigan. A truck to him was a piece of jewelry and he gave it the same care. Long hours through the mud never seemed to bother him. As long as he was driving he was happy. One day Captain Graham found him up to his knees, groping around in the mud in the motor pool, and asked him what he was doing.

"Only looking for the last wheel-lug wrench in the Battalion, sir," was his amiable reply. He found it, eventually.

Another problem pursued us now, too. The Division and attached troops were scheduled in the original plans of the operation to land on Guam and stay only long enough to secure the island, and then ship to—you guessed it, New Caledonia. The bigger part of our road—building equipment, our Special Service radios, athletic equipment, vehicles, pyramidal tents, cots—in fact, everything that would make for a better life—was awaiting our arrival on that island. All of our mail except airmail and V-mail was going there. We should be going there, too, but we weren't. Not just then. Somewhere there was a change in plans. In the meantime we heard no radio programs, we read no newspapers, we received no packages. PX supplies were obtainable in very limited amounts through the Navy. The men ran out of writing paper and envelopes and were furnished manifest sheets from the office supply stock. They made their own envelopes. The Red Cross helped with whatever it had. That wasn't much. Their supplies too, were going to New Caledonia. We ate C rations, K rations and Ten-in-One rations—all highly concentrated, salt-flavored packaged foods. The entire 77th was existing on the same diet. Soon after the island was declared secured and the mopping-up was completed for the moment, the Division had moved to a location south and east of the Battalion on the eastern slope of the small mountain range. Here on a beautiful slope they had bivouacked and named their camp, Camp McNair in honor of the late Chief of Staff of the Division who had been killed in action.

Soon the Division supply dumps had completed their move to Dadi Beach, and it appeared that now we might go off the 24-hour basis. We didn't.

Lieutenant Romaine S. Foss, Sergeant Robert F. Cater and Private Alfred W. Kruck, Jr., attended a Division Bomb Disposal School for three days. When they returned things began to explode. Their mission was to rid the Battalion area of any or all duds—unexploded missiles of varying sizes. It even became necessary to seek a foxhole on occasion during the next few days. They carefully loaded the duds, including a 5-inch naval shell, into the back of a jeep and hauled them over the hill occupied by the Battalion, and down into the ravine behind. Here they set them off with charges of TNT. Fragments whizzed over the area for a couple of days during the process, but soon the area was rid completely of the dangerous duds.

As soon as the 307th Combat Team moved into the Division area, Captain Robert K. Graham, the Battalion S-4, dispatched a water team to set up a water point in the vicinity of the Combat Team. Among the men operating this water point were Private First Class Alvin A. Card from Michigan, Private First Class Chester M. Dubaniewicz from Ohio, and Private First Class Joseph E. Goldsmith, Jr., and Private T. Pierce, ex-Alcan Highwayman, who told tall stories to keep lonelinesss from completely engulfing these men in their isolated situation. A squad from Company B was assigned the mission of protecting the water point. It was a primitive life for these men for the ensuing period, for the only

It was a primitive life.

contact they had with anyone was to talk to the drivers of the water trucks. The Operations Section felt they could spare the squad from Company B as Johnson Road would be no problem now. Lieutenant Romaine S. Foss was put on Special Duty with the newly formed Provisional Division Engineers Group Headquarters and left the Battalion for this assignment not to return until the 6th of December, 1944.

The 24-hour basis was not yet at an end. It never was. The rains washed out Harmon Road, the only accessible road to Camp McNair from Dadi Beach. This necessitated hand-carrying all rations and supplies up the three miles of hillside along Harmon Road. Again Johnson Road became the all-important supply route, for Companies B and C built a jeep trail from the end of the Company C road, over the mountain to Camp McNair. It was a jeep trail because it was so steep and narrow in places that it could accommodate only jeeps. The main supply route for the Division again traversed Johnson Road, and then continued over the jeep trail to the camp. Company A at this time was still working on Johnson Road keeping it open.

On the 5th of September the 77th Division and attached troops were again alerted for another operation. This time they were to participate in the Ulithi campaign. The 302d, 132d and 242d Engineer Battalions with the help of Company B, 233d Engineers, had been fighting hard to keep Harmon Road passable, and their

A jeep trail.

efforts had met with limited success. Light traffic was moving on Harmon Road and jeep traffic continued to move over the jeep trail, but to move the entire Division over the mountain to the beach was something else.

To move the tracked vehicles across country was out of the question, because of the deep ravines and bottomless marshes, and Harmon Road could be expected to carry only the wheeled traffic at best. The mission of hurriedly constructing a road for moving the tanks was assigned to the Battalion. After looking the situation over, the decision was made to cut a road over the hills from Camp McNair to the Battalion area and then again to use Johnson Road to the beaches. Companies B and C were given the job.

In a few days, working between rains, the road was completed except for a creek crossing. Care was taken during the construction not to put traffic on the road when it was muddy. At the creek crossing a fill was started from both sides working out to the middle, where a gap was left for the flow of water. Bridging materials were not available, and this stream supplied the water for the water point and the 36th Field Hospital.

Lieutenant Otto W. Mourek, then commanding Company B, had the men of his company stand by in their building of the fill. Late in the afternoon of the first day it didn't rain and the Battalion commander decided the road had dried enough to support the traffic. Upon getting this word Lieutenant Mourek had the men of Company B fill the gap, completely damming up the stream. Dozers worked from both sides pushing the dirt into the gap, and demolition charges were placed in the fill as the work progressed. In the meantime the 706th Tank Battalion had loaded and was standing in line at the fill. At 1800 the tanks started to move across the fill, over the newly constructed road and out across Johnson Road to the beach. Five hours later at 2300 when all the Division's tracked equipment had crossed the fill the men of Company B set off the demolition charges and opened up the fill, releasing the water that had dammed up behind it. The mission was completed. The tanks were on the beach and once again Johnson Road, the nightmare of the 233d on Guam, had served us well.

The Battalion then packed up and moved to what had been the prewar Piti Naval Base in Apra Harbor. The ships were already in the harbor, and the ship's platoons from the Battalions started loading. On the day before the convoy was scheduled to sail the operation was cancelled. The island of Yap in the Ulithi Atoll was to be by-passed. The equipment, already loaded, was unloaded and transported back to the Battalion area.

For the next month the Battalion waited—but not without something to occupy its time. The maintenance of Johnson Road continued, and Company C was assigned the job of clearing an area on the northern end of the island for the Army radio station. Lieutenant Harley T. Crawford was in charge of the job and assigned equipment and operators from the entire Battalion. While work progressed on this project contact was made with enemy stragglers hiding in the thick jungle-like undergrowth and, since they proved reluctant to surrender, they were killed. Lieutenant Crawford's men suffered no casualties during these encounters. The island had been declared secured and devoid of organized resistance on the 21st of August, 1944 but there were many Japanese soldiers hiding in the little-frequented areas on the island attempting sabotage and nuisance raids on the working parties. In January, months later, an article appeared in *Time* stating that 6,000 Japanese soldiers had been killed on Guam from September to the end of the year, in addition to the many captured.

During the previous few weeks some changes had been made among the officers of the Battalion. Captain Richard S. Stevick took command of Company A and Lieutenant Otto W. Mourek of B. Captain Clarence E. Johnson was now Battalion S-3 and Captain Roland D. Vandale the Assistant Division Engineer.

Towards the latter part of October the Division was again alerted. This time it was to move to the "Garden Spot of the Pa-

We got in while the going was rugged and moved out ahead of the USO shows.

cific"—none other than the, up to now mythical, New Caledonia. At long last we were going for rest and rehabilitation. Gardens had been growing all summer on New Caledonia, so rumor had it, and this meant fresh vegetables. There were cattle there, too— fresh meat, fresh milk and fresh butter. What a far cry that would be from the past and present! You can imagine with what zest the loading was accomplished. At last, the "Promised Land"! This time the convoy was commercially loaded, with the 233d on four different ships: the USS *Harris*, USS *Barnstable*, USS *Herald of the Morning* and the USS *Elmore*. They had come to Guam from Leyte, P.I., where they had put ashore elements of the troops now liberating the Philippines. The invasion there had just begun.

On the 2d of November, early morning, the convoy sailed from Apra Harbor, Guam, M.I., and headed east. We were leaving our first battleground. We had a completed campaign under our belts, a star in our Asiatic-Pacific Ribbon, but I'm sure no one left Guam with tears in his eyes. A lifetime on the Guam we had just left that morning with all its mud, rain, mosquitoes and rugged life didn't seem too attractive. In the next few months, however, the Seabees and Army Engineers built our strongest Middle Pacific Base on Guam. It was from there and Saipan that the B-29s carried destruction, and eventually the Atomic Bomb, to Japan. Our lot was not on advance bases then or in the future, however, because we always got in while the going was rugged and moved out ahead of the USO Shows and the opening dates of the Quartermaster Stores.

On the 15th of November, 1944 the convoy crossed the Equator. New Caledonia was straight ahead. In the tradition of the sea all Pollywogs crossing the Equator were inducted into the Order of Shellbacks. The men of the Battalion, all being Pollywogs, were recipients of a vehement initiation, much to the enjoyment of the Navy personnel present.

Again we had become accustomed to the loudspeaker's "Now hear this!" but we were doubly surprised one morning just two days out of New Caledonia to hear: "Now hear this! The orders have been changed. We are turning and heading into the Harbor of Manus Island in the Bismarck Archipelago. We will be moving through submarine-infested waters. All Army personnel will wear their life-jackets at all times." Nothing further was said about the change but everyone was trying to figure out what was coming. We had all been reading the daily news sheets the Navy Communications Section on every ship puts out. We knew from the reports that the Leyte campaign didn't look too good. The five Divisions now fighting there had driven the Japanese Army back into the Ormoc Corridor, but here the Jap had held. He was pouring thousands of reinforcements ashore at Ormoc and Palompon and the fighting there had developed into a major conflict, with the U.S. forces bogged down by the torrential rains.

We put into Manus Harbor for two days to take on supplies and readjust the loads. There it became evident we were going to Leyte. There was some fear running among the men of the Battalion now. Good soldiers are human; they get scared, too. The Japs still had a submarine base at Truk and we were going to pass in its vicinity. There also was a rumor that the Japanese Navy had a blockade across the entrance to Leyte Gulf and just the thought of another campaign, with the equipment we had with us shot and the men in a rundown condition, was not heartening. The bulk of our equipment was still awaiting our arrival at New Caledonia, along with all our packages from home and all our recreational equipment. The 233d was again going to war—this time more poorly equipped than before—but whatever the job was to be we could do it and do it well, equipment or no equipment.

CHAPTER VIII

LEYTE—AND A DEEPER MUDHOLE

On the morning of the 23d of November, 1944 the convoy dropped anchor near the town of Dulag, Leyte, Philippine Islands. The troops started landing at 0730 on another already established beach. We landed on Yellow One and Two at the town of Rizal, and unlike Guam, the beaches were sandy, with a high beating surf that hit the beach at an angle. During the unloading eight LCVPs and LCMs were capsized due to this unusual angling surf. The Shore Party Command Post was established midway between the two beaches and Major Orlan A. Johnson, the Battalion commander, was in command of all the unloading over these two points. Company A immediately began unloading the USS *Harris* and USS *Arneb*, Company B the USS *Elmore* and USS *Herald of the Morning* and Company C the *Barnstable*.

Dump areas were cleared, generators were set up in preparation for night work, and the separate companies soon had their individual shore parties organized. At the end of eight hours the first ship, the USS *Elmore*, was unloaded. At the end of sixteen hours the last ship had been unloaded, and the Battalion had put the entire 307th Combat Team on Leyte. The Infantry immediately moved inland to the vicinity of LaPaz, leaving working parties to assist with the moving of supplies and equipment inland to dumps.

It was here and now that the 233d cooks and mess sergeants showed that no matter what the job, they too could do it. By evening of that first day the kitchens were set up and operating. Captain Graham had discovered that we were just in time for B rations. You can cook B rations and serve them hot, and there were frozen meats available to round out the menus—but alas, the poor mess sergeants and cooks! For breakfast the second day they fed men until all they had prepared was gone and hungry GIs still came. At noon, they prepared over double the amount and still had to turn many hungry men away. That evening the crowd increased. The added hungry mouths were the men of the working parties, left behind on the beach to help in the Regimental Dumps with only C and K rations to eat. Nobody could blame them for falling in a chow line where hot food and coffee were being served. So the cooks and mess sergeants of the four company kitchens pitched in and for the next three days fed over five hundred men a meal at each kitchen, instead of the 170-odd that was their normal responsibility. The Battalion Supply Section drew, and the four company kitchens prepared and fed, 1,200 rations a day for the next three days.

Work continued on the beaches, progressing efficiently, and on the 27th of November the Battalion, less Company B, moved inland. Captain Roland D. Vandale, the Assistant Division Engineer, his section, and Company B were left on the beach to continue and finish up the work here.

Headquarters, H&S Company, and A Company rode into their bivouac area at LaPaz, little knowing how they were going to be returning over the same route two weeks later. Company C, attached to the 104th Engineer Combat Battalion, bivouacked on the Mayorog–LaPaz road about a mile inland from Mayorog. Camp was set up in both places and the native Filipinos swarmed in to do whatever they could to help their Americano cousins. Filipino guerrilla troops were stationed as outposts aiding our own perimeter guards. Company A was assigned the road from LaPaz to the CP of the 307th Infantry Regiment, and Company C was assigned road maintenance on a section of the access road to LaPaz. On the 3d of December Company B moved to the Battalion area, one mile inland from LaPaz.

Then the rains came. They continued to come. The 77th Division, with attached troops, was committed to the action on Leyte and assigned a special mission. The 233d was fighting frantically to keep the road from LaPaz to Mayorog open. It became an impossible job. The mud was from two to four feet deep along its entire length. Soon the road would be completely impassable unless the rains stopped. They didn't. Then the orders came for the 307th Regiment to move back to the beach. The LaPaz–Mayorog road was bordered by marshes and rice paddies, and the incessant tropical rains had softened the road until now it was one continuous mudhole from end to end.

The men of the Battalion worked like men never worked before. The 307th had to get out, and we had to get them through the mud. Work wasn't on a "24-hour basis" now; it was continuous until the job was done. If ever at any time during their overseas tour men and officers of the 233d came close to giving up, it was here on the LaPaz–Mayorog road. Coconut logs were cut and placed in the sea of mud. Dozers pulled vehicle after vehicle through the bottomless quagmire until they themselves were buried so deep they couldn't be pulled out, and were abandoned. Men waded and sloshed through knee-deep slush with tow chains, guiding logs into place, and at the end of four days and nights the 307th Infantry was on the beach some fifteen miles away. If Guam had been tough, this was unbelievable.

The Combat Team was down on the beach ready for the coming action, less the 233d Engineers who were buried in a gigantic mudhole fifteen miles inland. The Battalion commander reported that it would be impossible to get the Battalion equipment that was left out to the beach in time to leave with the convoy. Word came back that the 233d would be left behind, a casualty of the Philippine elements. Then Major Johnson waded, on foot, out to the beach, to be of any assistance he could in the loading. The 242d Engineers were on the beach to load the Division. Captain Clarence E. Johnson was placed temporarily in command of the Battalion and the companies were left digging out of the mud and repairing the few pieces of equipment they could salvage.

That night the .50-caliber machine gun directly in rear of the Battalion CP opened up. The gunner had seen movement in the undergrowth across his field of fire. Quickly the men of H&S, A and B companies moved into their prearranged defense position. Captain Nick Angel, the H&S Company commander, went straight to the gun position that had fired the warning of a night attack. After studying the situation from a prone position alongside the machine gun, he called for his men to follow him and moved forward.

The men moved across the clearing and into the jungle. After kicking around in the undergrowth and finding nothing they returned to the perimeter.

The next morning beamed with sunshine, a sort of glamorous climax to the previous weeks of rain. Everywhere blankets were hanging out to dry. Filipino women and girls were circulating through the camp, returning cleaned clothes to the soldiers. They would pick up the men's dirty mud-laden uniforms early in the morning, take them to nearby streams, and beat them between rocks until they were clean—sometimes until they were shreds. After they were dry the clothes would be returned the next morning. Price of our laundry? Twenty-five centavos—twelve and a half cents to you. This had been the daily routine since we had moved to LaPaz, and for mud soldiers, it was indeed a grand luxury. For once the men didn't have to scrub out their own mud- and grease-soaked field uniforms. The local carpenters had been hired to erect bamboo-framed shacks with palm-leaf sides and roof. They would split the bamboo stocks and put raised floors in their structures, and a man could get a dry night's sleep, if he wasn't working on the road that night.

Then came the order to move at once to the beach. The Battalion had been selected to go on the coming action. The equipment was left behind. Ten men from each company were left behind to guard it. Shortly after noon we were under way with Captain Clarence E. Johnson leading the column on a forced march to the beach fifteen miles away. In addition to their personal weapons, packs, ammunition and equipment, the men were sloshing along through the deepening mud, under a torrid sun, burdened down with machine guns, mortars, radios and the many things they would need when meeting the enemy. By nightfall the beach was reached. The men had been completely fatigued before the march, and the added torture of a blazing tropical sun, the labor of sloshing mile after mile, hour after hour, through the mud, carrying additional weight, was next to unbearable. However, not one man dropped out on that unforgettable march. They weren't afraid of the coming action; they were working hard to go along.

The night was spent borrowing equipment and drawing supplies, and on the morning of the 6th of December, 1944 the Battalion, ragged, tired and verging on discouragement, boarded LCIs. The equipment—dozers, vehicles, etc.—had been borrowed from the 242d Combat Engineers, then working on the beach loading the troops and equipment for the movement.

At about dusk on the evening of the 6th, the Battalion's rear echelon, consisting of forty men commanded by Captain Robert K. Graham, assisted by Lieutenant Allen K. Reid, was preparing to spend the night in the neighborhood of LaPaz, which was now deserted by our Army. Several large transport planes approached from the mountains to the west. They appeared to be friendly planes, and the men, thinking them our own, continued with their work. Minutes later the planes roared overhead at about two hundred feet. It was then that the men saw the large orange Rising Suns on the wings. It was then they saw Japanese paratroopers bailing out and dropping into the Company C area. The Japs hit the ground with a thud and came up face to face with a handful of fighting engineers. The struggle was short but fierce, and the Japanese soldiers left a number of their party strewn around over the Company C area. Men from the anti-aircraft positions in the immediate area came to the assistance of the Engineers and the remnants of the Jap forces were driven off into the jungle. There were more Japanese landing in the adjacent areas, and while this little band of men had killed or driven off those landing in their immediate area, the situation was precarious. These Jap paratroopers had brand-new equipment, and carried a maximum amount of fire power and demolitions. Staff Sergeant Harry E. McDaniels was killed in the hand-to-hand struggle. Privates First Class John J. Downes and Oscar A. Coleman and Privates Gilbert T. Owens and Robert A. St. Marys were wounded by enemy action.

Lieutenant Reid, at the time at Division Rear Echelon Headquarters on the beach, was attempting to get a message through to Captain Graham. At Headquarters they had heard of the attack and realized the situation of this handful of men. Since the paratroopers had the detachment cut off, Lieutenant Reid boarded a reconnaissance plane, flew over the area, and dropped the message to Captain Graham in an ammunition box. Upon receipt of the message, ordering him to abandon all equipment and get his men through to the beach at once, Captain Graham could see only two possible ways to accomplish this mission: either to abandon all equipment and sneak his crippled force through to the beach, or to make a bold attempt to save the equipment. He chose the latter course. As the road had dried up considerably in the last two days of bright sunshine, he loaded the men on the trucks and dozers, and with all lights turned on and the men making as much noise as possible, thereby attempting to deceive the enemy into thinking that a large force was passing through they started for the beach. They were successful. This small band of men, isolated and trapped in the midst of the enemy paratroop attack, through the quick actions of Lieutenant Allen K. Reid and the leadership of Captain Robert K. Graham, successfully met the attack and courageously removed valuable equipment from the inevitable destruction planned by the enemy.

CHAPTER IX

ORMOC—A NAME TO REMEMBER

The news stories all glorified the famous "End Run" to the assault of enemy-held beaches a few miles south of Ormoc, on Leyte. They told of the orderly landing of supplies and then troops; of the movement, under cover of darkness, around the southern end of the island; the early morning bombardment, and the soldiers hitting the beach at 0707, because the General liked sevens for his 77th. Pictures were published of assault craft on the Ormoc Beachhead, the supplies and vehicles being hauled ashore and men working—up to their knees—waist—chins—in salt water, passing ammunition, rations, supplies, supplies and more supplies ashore. The men they wrote about, working in water up to their chins, passing supplies ashore on the Omoc Beachhead, were the Engineers of the 233d, the sole Shore Party for the 77th Infantry Division on this daring amphibious move on the third anniversary of Pearl Harbor.

Notwithstanding the fact that the beach was under fire, the Battalion assumed its assigned work of organizing and defending the 700-yard beach immediately upon landing. During the progress of the work the enemy continued to harass the beach with machine-gun and small-arms fire. Enemy mortar shells fell spasmodically on the southern sector of the beach, operated by Company C, under the command of Captain Christian C. Lutz. The beach as a whole served as an impact area for enemy fire directed at the infantry expanding the beachhead inland. However, with six dozers and two small cranes, the Battalion unloaded the Division Task Force, including four days' supplies, in the first four hours after landing. Thus, the convoy was relieved to retract from the beach and get underway before the first enemy air strike, which came at H plus four-and-one-half hours. The complete convoy consisted of 26 LCIs, 12 LSMs and 4 LSTs.

The first enemy planes appeared at eleven thirty. Except for three LSMs, broached on the beach, the convoy was putting out to sea. They had said this was not going to be a Dunkirk. We had landed in the enemy's rear, splitting the Yamashita Line that ran from Limon, on the northern end of the island, to Baybay, fifteen miles to the south. If the enemy was strong enough to

Up to their knees . . . waists . . . chins . . . in salt water.

drive us off the newly established beachhead, it would be into the sea, for there was no place else to go. The convoy that had brought us had left as quickly as it was unloaded, taking their escorts with them. Our closest contact with friendly forces was through fifteen miles of enemy-held territory to the south where the 7th Division was driving hard to meet us. They had jumped off on a gigantic push the day before. We had established a beachhead with sixty thousand Japanese soldiers on three sides and the open sea on the other.

The men of the Battalion were busy on an access road, inland to the hard-surface highway half a mile away. This was an easy task as the soil was quite sandy and no rain was yet falling. The beach dumps were organized, and aside from dodging mortar shells and sniper fire, most of the men were free at this time to improve their foxholes and eat K rations. Captain Robert K. Graham's water men were installing a waterpoint on a stream that bordered the beachhead on the south. The beach had been divided into two sections, called White Beach One and White Beach Two. During the unloading Company C had worked the southern half, White Two, and Company A the north, White One. Company B had been split between the two beaches. H&S Company had helped to organize the Shore Party CP consisting of a large tree, under which was dug a series of foxholes. The switchboard and radios had been set up underground and contact had been made with the companies and Division Headquarters. Captain Roland D. Vandale and his assistant, Staff Sergeant Carmen N. Muratore, were up towards the front at the hastily established Division CP. H&S Company men had also been instrumental in helping the medical detachment establish the Beachhead Aid Station. An occasional wounded soldier was being brought to the beach from the troops fast advancing inland and turning north towards Ormoc. First Sergeant Jack J. Johnson had established a protective line about fifty yards inland in rear of the Cp, and this time Lieutenant Otto W. Mourek, with the assistance of his Platoon Commanders, Lieutenant Byron C. Hanson, John Hude, Jr., Peter J. Langhans, and William W. Lassetter, were extending this protective line both north and south along the entire length of the beachhead.

Suddenly tracers began to fill the air to the north of the Beachhead, and by the time our own .50-caliber machine guns had swung into position, facing the oncoming planes, the two Japanese bimotored bombers (Sallys) were bearing down on the beach at a height of approximately seven hundred feet. A combination of 40mm. antiaircraft fire (we had four AA guns on the beach) and a .30- and .50-caliber machine-gun fire was delivered at the attacking planes. One dived flaming into the sea approximately fifty yards in front of the Battalion CP, the other, completing his first run without dropping his bombs, circled around and made another run at the beach. He met with the same fate as the first, splashing just off shore, in front of Company A.

Immediately after the first air attack, the three broached LSMs helped by the rising tide, got off the beach and headed out to sea to the south in an attempt to overtake the convoy already en route to the east side of Leyte. When perhaps three miles south and west, on their route in wake of the convoy, which by then was out of sight, these three LSMs met with the second air attack of the day. There were five planes in the attack. Three U.S. Army P-38s appeared out of nowhere amid loud cheering and yelling from the beach, and immediately dropped four of the attackers in the drink. The men on the beaches felt better. The fifth Japanese plane suicide-dived into one of the LSMs, setting it afire and sinking it. The other two LSMs picked up the survivors of the sunken ship and returned to the beach. Men were dispatched from H&S Company, with litters, to board the craft as they dropped their gates and to get the wounded sailors to the aid station for medical treatment.

Just as these litter-bearers were boarding the first LSM, the third air attack came. This was a lone bomber, flying very low, from the north. All the guns on the beach and the LSM threw up a terrific amount of lead at the oncoming plane. The litter-bearers continued into the ship and loaded the wounded sailors. An LSM is an open-topped landing craft, and while the sides afford some protection, a bomb dropped so as to land on the deck would be disastrous. When over Company A's section of the beach, and about four hundred yards from the LSM, the attacking plane burst into flame. Everyone on the beach at this moment was digging in deep, except the gunners from their protected positions and the men from H&S Company who had just emerged from the front of the ship and started down the ramp with their wounded charges. The determined Jap pilot intended to take all with him that he could so he nosed his flaming plane directly at the LSM. His .50s were spitting fire, and the bullets were clanging as they hit the steel of the ship.

Men yelled to the litter-bearers to take cover. The litter-bearers ignored the warning. Those wounded sailors they were carrying came first, and they continued on their way, wading to the beach and rushing into the grove of trees surrounding the aid station. The names of these gallant men, litter-bearers from H&S Company, are not all known and none is mentioned here, but it is this kind of complete disregard for self in the face of certain danger that puts the American soldier in the top rank among fighting men. Here were heroes. Regrettably, because their identity was lost in the confusion, they must go without formal reward. Their fellow soldiers, those on the beach who saw the deed, hold the highest admiration and praise for these Engineers' courageous devotion to duty and their fellow men.

Seconds later the enemy plane splashed in the water, not ten feet from the LSM. It had caused some damage. As soon as the second LSM beached, the commanders of the two craft decided to wait at the beach until nightfall before trying the unescorted 225-mile run back to the east side of the island. A later report brought the good news that they had made the trip successfully.

Air attacks continued at frequent intervals throughout the

day. Captain Julius J. Simon and the medical aid men worked feverishly through it all on the open beachhead, caring for the wounded—GI and sailor alike. During the first day a total of fourteen enemy aircraft was shot down by the fire from the beach. Although the 233d received no actual credit for planes destroyed, it is the private opinion of those who were present that the Battalion's own .50-caliber guns took their toll, for the men who manned these guns were on target all day long.

Normally, the mission of organizing, operating, and defending the beaches for a divisional task-force landing is assigned to three Engineer Combat Battalions, and attached troops of a Joint Assault Signal Company who handle all communications. However, on this occasion, not only was this mission successfully accomplished in record time by one battalion and its attached JASCO personnel, but by nightfall on D-day, a second beachhead had been established and supplies were being moved north along the coast, keeping pace with the rapid advance of the infantry. Company B had been withdrawn from the inland protective line, leaving Companies A and C to form their own perimeter defense, and had moved a mile north along the coast line and established a second beachhead named Red Beach, at the newly captured town of Desposito. The infantry dug in for the night three-quarters of a mile north of Company B, approximately a quarter of a mile south of the town of Ipil, an enemy stronghold. In these positions, arranged over a mile and a half of coast line, the Battalion dug in for the night, with Company C as rear guard for the Task Force, being at the extreme south end of the original beachhead. During the night, mortar fire fell in the Company C area, wounding Sergeant Francis F. Walker of that company.

To insure the success of the operation it was imperative for the infantry to press swiftly northward toward Ormoc against a surprised enemy. Because of the lack of sufficient troops to leave behind for the protection of the beachhead, it became necessary to move the beachhead northward with the infantry advance. The progress of this work was continually hampered by enemy aircraft strafing and bombing the entire length of the beaches. However, by 1300 on the second day, the 8th of December, a third beachhead was finally established at Ipil. In addition to the work of moving the supplies and equipment to the two advanced beaches, elements of the 233d had defended the coastal sector of the beachhead to the south, effectively repelling enemy infiltrations under moderate mortar fire; had successfully defended the beaches to the seaward and from inland infiltration during the night; and Company B, moving from Red Beach, had landed from the sea in amtracks south of the railroad pier at Ipil, assisting the infantry in their attack on that town. During the morning Headquarters, H&S, and A Companies had followed Company B, and upon their arrival at Ipil proceeded to clear the town of booby-traps and enemy stragglers that were harassing the work on the beach by firing intermittently from their hideouts amid the debris. By 1400 that afternoon, the 8th of December, all supplies had been moved to the beachhead at Ipil from the two southern beaches. At this time the Division's supplies were in front of the Regimental supply sections, greatly assisting the advance of the infantry, as the supplies were available practically at the front lines.

Enemy air strikes continued until dark and upon occasion the work on the beaches was completely stopped by enemy machine guns firing from the high ground approximately one thousand yards inland from Ipil. Sniper fire also proved aggravating to the men working on the beach during the afternoon.

Later in the afternoon, the area between the coastline and Highway Number Two, reaching from the 233d's northern defense position at Ipil Beachhead, north to the river bordering Camp Downs on the south, was open to the enemy. This area presented a threat to the left flank of the Division troops, holding a line at the foot of the hill below Camp Downs. Upon receipt of orders from the Division Company B was sent to clear out the area. About two hours before dark, when the order had arrived, Company B moved out. They advanced northward through the designated area, eliminated all enemy troops, and returned to the beachhead perimeter by dark, where they dug in for the night in a defensive position.

Company C remained in its original position at the extreme southern end of the original beachhead. Spasmodic mortar fire again fell through the night in the Company C area.

It was Bronze Arrowhead and another Star for the men of the 233d. They had made their first landing on an enemy-held beach, established a beachhead, moved it twice in the first two days, had been bombed and shot at plenty, and had shot back plenty. That "can do" attitude had become automatic now. The jobs didn't come too big for the Griffins. If no one else knew it, they knew that they had broken records and had met with great success in their accomplishments on the beachhead at Ormoc.

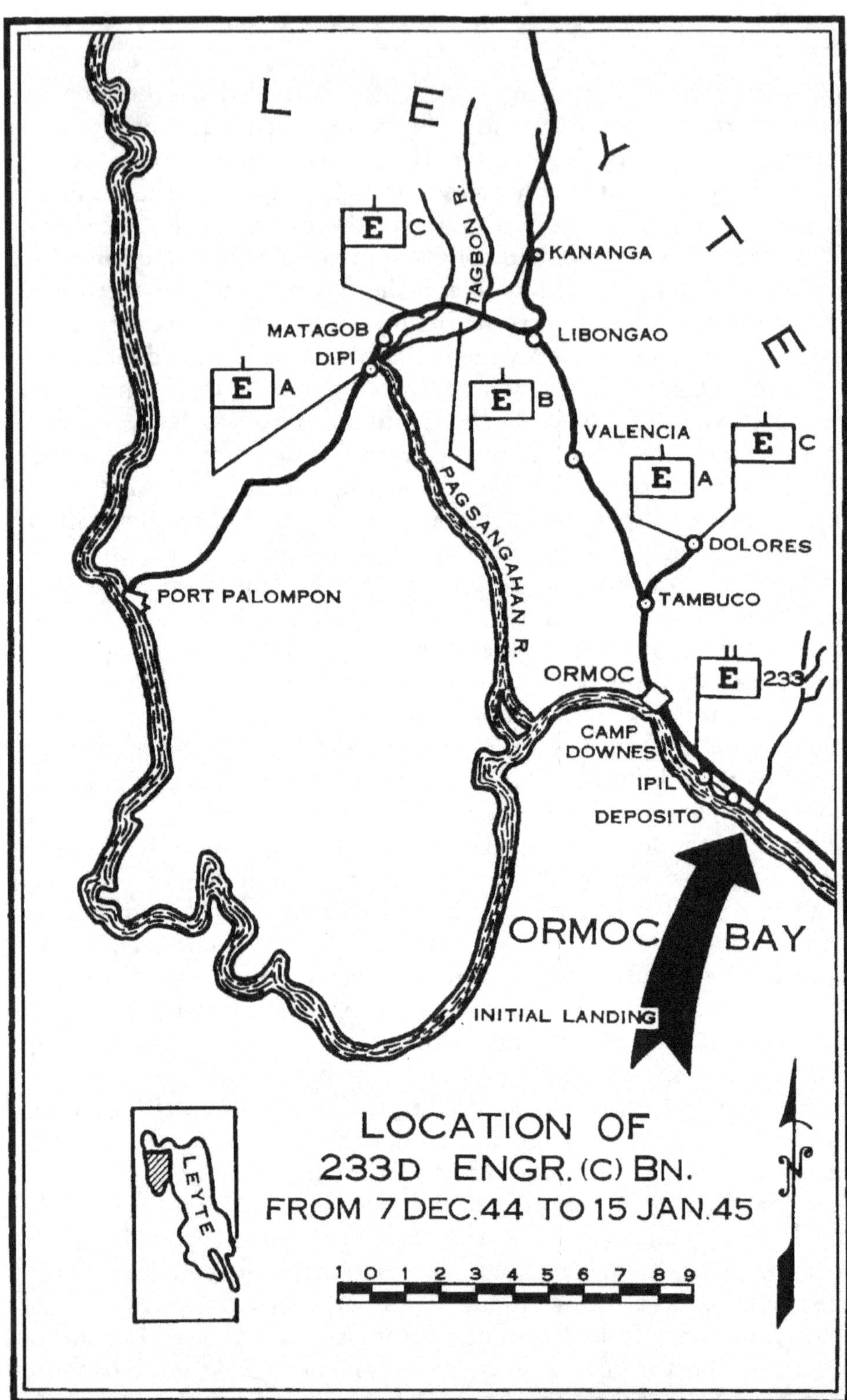

LEYTE
E C
KANANGA
TAGBON R.
MATAGOB
DIPI
LIBONGAO
E A
E B
VALENCIA
E C
E A
DOLORES
PORT PALOMPON
PAGSANGAHAN R.
TAMBUCO
ORMOC
E 233
CAMP DOWNES
IPIL
DEPOSITO
ORMOC BAY
INITIAL LANDING
LEYTE
LOCATION OF
233D ENGR. (C) BN.
FROM 7 DEC. 44 TO 15 JAN. 45
1 0 1 2 3 4 5 6 7 8 9
N

CHAPTER X

TURKEY FOR CHRISTMAS

There had been precious little sleep for the Griffins. The first night had been clear and dry, with a bright moon, but the second night ashore was a completely successful rainy night. It poured in torrents. The men, submerged in their foxholes, spent the night watching and waiting. Would the Jap try to drive them out? The men didn't think much of their present location, but if the Jap came he'd find it would be tough to root them out. They had established a lease of sorts on that location and they intended to stay.

The night finally wore itself out without any serious action from the enemy, and the men welcomed the morning. At least they could get above ground and stretch their water-soaked, aching legs. A bit of hot coffee would do nicely, too, if they could find something dry to build a fire to heat water. No attempts had been made to set up the kitchens and the men were still eating K and C rations.

The first resupply convoy arrived at 0630, coming around the southern end of the island at night to avoid enemy attacks. It consisted of seven LSMs and four LCIs carrying twelve hundred tons of cargo and some more troops. Due to a threatened air strike, the convoy commander ordered the convoy off the beach at 0810, one hour and fifty minutes after reaching it. The men of the Battalion had unloaded ninety per cent of the cargo, but the battle casualties of the past two days, lying there on the beach on litters ready to be loaded, were left behind. Later in the day a convoy of LCMs from the Third Engineer Amphibious Brigade at Baybay evacuated these litter cases to a hospital near that town, making the thirty-mile round trip along the coast unescorted.

Company C moved to Ipil beachhead and the rest of the day was spent in cleaning up the beach and the town of Ipil. Thatched huts and wreckage were burned, areas were cleared for dumps and a cemetery, and graves were dug for the dead of the division and attached troops. The beach was cleared of eighteen sunken or abandoned Japanese barges.

Air raids continued, mostly one-plane attacks. There was an Army Air Corps umbrella of fighter planes overhead now most of

Later in the day, a convoy of LCMs evacuated these litter cases.

the day. Still occasional lone planes would skim in over the trees, the shells from their strafing kicking up the sand on the beach as they raced along. You could see these shells walk right up the beach at you and then go on down the beach past you, and somehow, miraculously miss you. As soon as the strafing was over the men always got up to see where the pilot was going to try to place his bombs. There were always two bombs and the pilot would kick the plane into a turn, loosing the bombs at his target at the same time. Some drifted out and landed in the ocean at the edge of the beach and others dropped along the beach or in a bivouac area. These bombs didn't do too much damage as they were usually small, but occasionally one hit in a vital spot. One of these bombs, late the afternoon of the 9th of December, landed between the Company B and Company C areas, wounding nine men and killing Private First Class Richard Forbes of Company C.

After these first three days and nights, the war began to show among the ranks of the 233d. The horseshoe luck was still holding out—but for how long? The animosity of the men towards the Japanese soldier was becoming a fierce obsession. To them the Jap had become nothing more than an animal to be stamped out of existence. War had long since passed the adventure stage. It was dangerous and destructive. There was no pleasure to be derived from war or even from being in the Pacific Islands. There was little you could do. Keep going, do the job well, and maybe some day if you were lucky you'd get home after this was all over—or maybe sooner you would take the longer route home if you were wounded.

At 0430 that morning, the convoy left, preferring to get off the beach and on its way before daybreak.

By the fifth day of the operation, the 11th of December, Division dumps were being established in Ormoc. The bleach-head was to remain at Ipil, as the harbor at Ormoc could not be used. The five bridges on the highway between Ipil and Ormoc were repaired and strengthened by Company C. The next night one of the five was dynamited by a Japanese patrol, and it became necessary to place guards on these bridges.

During the first half of that night the Battalion prepared for a night seaward attack, which, with the aid of the 7th Anti-aircraft Battalion (Automatic Weapons) was beaten off. The second resupply convoy arrived just past midnight. At the same time, Japanese ships were standing off in the harbor, across by the peninsula that extended south from Ormoc. A Japanese landing craft had been salvaged by the men in the motor pool, and the Battalion had been using it along the beach. An American flag was made from Japanese silk by Captain Theodore C. Meinelt, the battalion S-2, and "USA" was painted on both sides of the landing craft with white paint. This was to prevent the batteries along the coast from mistaking it for a Japanese-manned boat and firing upon it. Lieutenant Rondo W. Ruesch agreed to take Major DePetro, representative of the 1118th Engineer Com-bat Group, out to the flagship of our resupply convoy in this now converted Japanese landing craft. With Staff Sergeant Robert F. Brelsford and Technician Fourth Grade Howard J. Green, both of Company B, operating the boat, they were to go out to the convoy with information as to the condition of the beach and to guide the convoy in.

As the pilot boat drew near the convoy, it was caught in the sudden brilliance of a searchlight beam, which it was soon discovered, came from a Japanese ship. Upon seeing the American flag flying from the stern of the boat, the Japanese ship immediately began firing. The ships in our convoy began to return the fire. Then from somewhere out of the night, unidentified planes began strafing the area of the sea battle. To the watchers on the beach, the picture was somewhat confused and a feeling ran through everyone that the improvised pilot boat and its crew were lost. However, after about fifteen minutes the firing stopped, and the motors of approaching boats were heard on shore. The brilliant display of fireworks having ceased, the night was black, and the men on the beach spent some breathless minutes peering out to sea, trying to determine whether approaching craft were our own convoy or Japanese landing craft. At 0055, the dark hulls of LSMs appeared. The craft then scraped to a stop at the water's edge. The pilot boat had guided the convoy safely into the beach.

For their heroic actions the men who had courageously operated the pilot boat were awarded the Bronze Star Medal. At 0430 that morning the convoy left, preferring to get off the beach and on its way before daybreak, when enemy air attacks were certain to come. During the three hours and forty-five minutes of darkness that the LSMs had been at the beach, the Battalion had carried ashore nine hundred tons of bulk cargo, at the same time defending the flanks of the beachhead and guarding the five bridges on the road to Ormoc.

To sum up the beach operations of the Battalion: in the first five days, and in addition to the initial convoy of which the tonnage is unknown, 1008 tons of cargo had been unloaded from the two resupply convoys in five hours and thirty-five minutes; a total (including the initial convoy) of 308 vehicles, had been beached using only six dozers to pull them ashore through the surf and sand; eighteen LCMs from Baybay, with a total load of 185 tons of cargo had been unloaded over the beach at Ipil;

and 558 casualties had been evacuated over the beach and into LCMs to be taken to the hospital at Baybay.

On the night of the 21st of December the 3d Platoon of Company C, commanded by Lieutenant Thomas G. Blair, had drawn the bridge guard detail on the five bridges on the road to Ormoc. The squad leaders, knowing that daylight would bring another resupply convoy and that their men would go direct from the all-night bridge-guarding job to the vigorous job of unloading, had arranged their men in shifts. Half of the men would be on duty at a time, and the other four could try to get some sleep. Bridge-guarding was not new to the men of the 3d Platoon, Company C. They were veterans. But, bridge-guarding was a nerve-wracking job. There you were, six or eight men, dug in at a bridge, maybe only a half a mile or maybe two, or even three, miles from friendly troops. You lay there in your foxhole, peering into the night, thinking, wondering, hoping the night would pass without incident. You'll not find six or eight men anywhere who like to be alone, pitted against an unknown number of enemy soldiers in the darkness, but this was their job. Tomorrow night it would be other men, the next night still others, and so on until your turn came again. This wasn't like being in a company or platoon on the front lines slugging it out in the daylight, with artillery, tanks and automatic weapons in your support. This was sheer loneliness coupled with hours of anticipation, expecting trouble, outnumbered, away from immediate help, alone with your buddies in the stillness of the night. Trouble seldom came, but this night it did.

Sergeant Michael J. Rawlins had his men on Bridge Number Four. He, with Privates Lloyd W. Shellenbarger, Robert Goulet and Private First Class William B. Ide, Jr., were on shift. Private First Class Floyd B. Seivers and the other three members of the squad were a little distance away, dug in and sleeping. Near 2300, Shellenbarger saw what appeared to be four men approaching the position across the bridge.

He cried "Halt!" His challenge was answered with grenades.

The bursts killed Shellenbarger and the squad leader, Sergeant Rawlins. Private First Class Ide, severely wounded, crawled from his cover across to the machine gun, removed Shellenbarger, who had fallen over the gun, and started firing at the enemy. The next instant, upon hearing a cry from Goulet, he whipped the gun around, firing over Goulet, who was being attacked from behind, and killed the attacking Jap soldier. From loss of strength caused by his wounds, Ide then collapsed, falling over the gun with his finger still pulling the trigger. The surviving member, Goulet, although severely wounded in the back, crawled over to the gun and began sweeping the area in the direction of the enemy. Private First Class Seivers, awakened by the melee, left his place of concealment and dashed over to assist the four men. He took the gun as Goulet collapsed and drove off the remaining enemy. Satisfied that the enemy had dispersed, he ran through the woods, even though he was fully aware of lurking enemy in the vicinity, to a command post over half a mile away and borrowed a jeep. Driving back to the bridge, he loaded the two wounded men, Ide and Goulet, into the jeep and drove them to the hospital at Ormoc. Returning the jeep to the command post, he once again made his way, alone, through the woods to the bridge. At the Battalion area Captain Christian C. Lutz, hearing the firing and realizing it was coming from the bridge guarded by his men, dispatched a platoon to the scene.

For his courageous action and devotion to duty, Private First Class William B. Ide, Jr., was awarded the Silver Star Medal and Private First Class Floyd B. Seivers and Private Robert Goulet were awarded the Bronze Star Medal.

The convoy arriving at dawn the next morning had, in addition to its other cargo, two huge refrigerated semitrailers loaded with turkey. The 77th Division Task Force, right in the middle of the final stages of the Leyte Campaign, was going to have turkey for Christmas. The Quartermaster had certainly come through for us. However, on the 24th of December the Battalion was ordered to turn the beach over to the other engineer battalion that had arrived and to move up to the front lines on the Libungao–Palompon Road north of Valencia.

"What about the turkey?"

"Oh, the Mess Sergeants already have it."

"How can they cook it on the move?"

"Aren't we going to have our turkey on Christmas Day?" The men, all asking questions such as these, were more concerned about having turkey on Christmas Day than they were that the 233d was being ordered to the front lines for the first time. That didn't seem to worry anyone any more. They had a few personal scores to settle with the Jap Army.

CHAPTER XI

TANKS TO DIPPI

Company A moved out as soon as it could load and began the 11-mile run to Valencia. While the area along the road from Ormoc to Valencia had been covered by the infantry during its advance, there had been no troops left behind to occupy this area. Supplies were moved by armored convoy from the dumps at Ormoc to troops up front over this single supply route. The 307th Infantry had established a strongpoint at Valencia to protect the airfield captured there. To get to the front-line area the convoys, each company forming its own, had to make the 8-mile jump from Ormoc to Valencia with guns bristling from every truck. They then proceeded north along the highway to the Libungao Junction, which was still steaming from battle, and turned west along the Palompon road to cross through the battlefield, still strewn with numerous Japanese dead, to a little town named Dippi. Dippi was immediately behind the foot soldiers of the 305th Infantry, then spearheading the drive to the west.

Lieutenant Allen K. Reid, the Battalion Reconnaisance Officer, preceded the convoys, alone in his jeep, to the battlefield area where he located bivouac areas for the companies. During his tour Lieutenant Reid chanced upon two enemy stragglers hiding out in a foxhole and sniping at passing traffic. These he disposed of at once in the usual manner and thereby earned the name among his buddies, of "Combat Reid, the Terror of the Battalion." Lieutenant Reid was of small stature and the name was very fitting. After the episode he proceeded on his mission, and upon the arrival of the companies, directed them to their camping areas.

Company A, under the leadership of Captain Richard S. Stevick, reached its bivouac area, a point immediately behind the front lines in the village of Dippi. They were greeted by Japanese 77mm. gunfire, and for the next half hour were forced to lie flat on the ground beside their trucks until the barrage subsided. Luckily, there were no casualties. The men immediately began to dig in, and shortly thereafter the company CP was established on the side of a small hill. Radio communication was established with Battalion headquarters, still on the beach some twenty miles away.

Our job was to repair, rebuild, or reinforce these twenty-six bridges.

Company C, their replacements for the job on the beach having arrived, started their move to the front shortly after noon, under the command of Captain Christian C. Lutz. After traversing the dangerous Ormoc–Valencia strip of their route, they were held up overnight at a roadblock just north of Valencia, and continued their move the following morning to their bivouac area some three miles down the road from Company A. Here, on a knoll, their camp was set up.

During the night Company A had been under considerable artillery fire from the enemy in the mountains to the west. The men of the company, however, even though spending Christmas Eve in foxholes, had successfully tuned the company radio in on a station in French Indo-China and listened to Christmas carols which, although they were sung in French, served momentarily to take their minds off the war.

Early Christmas morning, the forward headquarters detachment, the Medical Detachment, and Headquarters Platoon of Company B moved out separately for their camp at the front lines. Upon arriving at the Tagabon River, they immediately began to set up the Battalion forward CP and the Company B area. The remainder of Company B was to arrive later in the day but they too met with a roadblock and were forced to wait along the road and continue their move the following morning. That night on the Tagabon River will be one not soon forgotten by the men of Headquarters and Company B who were present. Being alone and miles from the closest troops, and few in number, all officers

When morning came the bridge was finished.

and men present were formed into a perimeter. The Tagabon River served as a highway for the enemy trapped between the 77th Division and the 1st Cavalry Division who were pressing in farther north, and the section to the south still held by enemy troops. The men stayed in their foxholes, controlling their fire, but continually throughout the night infiltrating enemy troops moved around the area and down the Tagabon.

The Christmas turkey dinner was served to the men of the Battalion on the 26th of December, but most of them realized that it was the same time the folks back home were indulging, because the Battalion was west of the International Date Line.

Immediately upon arrival in their new positions the various elements of the Battalion had started right in on the job at hand. There were twenty-six bridges, or at least streams to be crossed, between Libungao Junction and the foot of the mountains to the west. Our job was to repair, rebuild or reinforce these twenty-six bridges so that they would carry the tanks across to the front lines. That meant that each bridge would have to support thirty-five tons or more. There was no material available for the job, but it had to be done. The situation was thoroughly explained to the men. It was imperative that the work be accomplished as quickly as possible. The Division had given us, at the most, five days and nights to do the job. The tanks had to get to the front lines, where the 305th Infantry, which was spearheading the drive to the west, was being held up for lack of armored guns to destroy the embedded enemy positions in the mountains west of Dippi.

Thus, the Griffins pitched in on a seemingly impossible mission. There were no supplies available to do the job. They had a five-day deadline. Yet, with their "Can Do" attitude they did it. They salvaged material from Filipino shacks and structures. They worked day and night, even ignoring the presence of the enemy to the extent of using lights at night on the bridges. They cut down trees, hewed timbers, wrecked shacks and small buildings, drove piling, nailed on runners, constructed stringers and installed braces. They built bridges, twenty-six of them, sometimes under enemy fire, often interrupted by enemy patrol action, but they built those bridges. On occasions, it became necessary for the platoons of Company A, under the direct leadership and driving power of Sergeants Charles E. Marquis and Ralph LaPorte, to work not over a hundred feet behind the immediate front lines on a newly taken bridge on the road to Palompon.

Clarence E. Johnson, the Battalion Operations Officer, accompanied by Captain Richard S. Stevick and Lieutenant George W. Gray, Jr., of Company A, on numerous occasions made trips out in front of the infantry advanced lines to estimate what would be necessary to fix the next bridge. They wanted to have the material ready so that when the infantry took the bridge they could start working on it immediately. Five days to build twenty-six bridges—and the Griffins were doing it.

Sergeants Merrill Blackman, David H. Flanders, Peter A. DeBlonk and Carmen N. Muratore of Headquarters, and Sergeants Gerald L. Kock, James J. Biebighauser, Dominic A. Pelowski and Daniel V. Bostrom of the line companies, and many other NCOs of the Battalion were working around the clock. They scoured the surrounding areas for material, timbers, and buildings to salvage material from. The line-company sergeants kept the work going on and on and on. Bridges were taking shape. Back on the first sector of the road, assigned to Company B, Lieutenants Byron C. Hanson, John Hude, Jr., Peter J. Langhans, and William W. Lassetter had successfully directed the construction of a number of the bridges. The tanks were beginning to move up, waiting until a bridge was finished, and then moving on to the next.

They were going to make it. Come what may they were going

to get the tanks through on time. On one trip out into the jungle in quest of materials, Sergeant Peter A. DeBlonk, Sergeant David H. Flanders and Private First Class Alfred W. Kruck, Jr., came upon three Filipino huts in a small clearing. Being some three hundred yards from anywhere, and with only three men, they decided to proceed with caution. At the edge of the clearing, Sergeant Flanders threw a hand grenade through the window of the nearest shack. Startled Japanese soldiers began to pour out of the other two huts. With a tommy gun, a carbine, and a rifle the three began to pour lead into the enemy. Later Private First Class Kruck said he had always figured that when you had done the job you were sent overseas to do, you would get yours. As he watched those Jap soldiers fall like clay pigeons in a shooting gallery, he thought the time had come. He admitted that he knew of one soldier who was scared, because he figured that he would never get back. In addition to the three Japs killed by the grenade in the first house, there were seven more lying just outside the entrance to the other two and the three huts were now ready for the salvage crews to start work on. The studs and joists of the Filipino huts were constructed from seasoned mahogany and became very useful in the job at hand.

On the last day there was one bridge, in the Company A sector, that hadn't yet been started on. It was still in front of the front lines when they dug in that night. Lieutenant George W. Gray, Jr., was assigned the job of reinforcing that bridge. As he passed through the infantry perimeter into no-man's land with his platoon that evening to accomplish the job, he was warned by the infantry captain that if trouble developed he was to get his men into the bottom of the stream bed and lie low because he, the infantry captain, could not hold his fire and take the chance of the enemy breaking through. With this in mind, Lieutenant Gray and the men of his platoon set to work on the bridge. When morning came the bridge was finished, as were all the other of the twenty-six. It was the 30th of December, the morning of the sixth day since the elements of the battalion had arrived at Dippi. The tanks went through. That day the Battalion moved back to the beach at Ipil.

Although the island had been declared secure when the 306th Infantry had landed at Palompon, it had meant nothing to the men of the 233d. They had seen one of the toughest jobs of their Pacific tour in the five days and nights on the road to Palompon.

CHAPTER XII

REST CAMP

On New Year's Day Companies A and C were ordered to Tambuco, at the junction of the Ormoc–Valencia road and the Dolores road. A bivouac was set up one mile east of the junction on the Dolores road. The mission was to maintain the Ormoc–Valencia road, the main supply route for the Division, and to guard its seven bridges. This also necessitated considerable patroling throughout the area adjacent to the bridges and Tambuco. In addition to these jobs, Staff Sergeant Gerald C. Kock later to be commissioned in the field to the grade of second lieutenant, was assigned the mission of constructing a four-span, 45-ton timber trestle bridge on the river just at the north edge of Ormoc. This was the first time that regular bridge timbers had been available. With his platoon and the assistance of Sergeant Tovia A. Rajala, Sergeant Kock successfully completed the bridge in record time.

While in the Tambuco area, patrols were continually sent over the area, and enemy snipers and infiltrators were just as continually eliminated. The 706th Tank Battalion assigned two tanks, one to each company, to be used in the event of attacks on the bridges or the bivouac areas. The two companies alternated, each furnishing the bridge guard every other night. In the intervening days the companies would furnish the bivouac guard and patrols.

On the night of the 8th of January, 1945 Company A was called out to investigate a Japanese roadblock between Tambuco and Valencia. During the ensuing action Technician Fifth Grade Roy A. Killam was killed and Captain Richard S. Stevick, Sergeant Leroy G. Reason, Technician Fifth Grade Jesse D. Guyer, and Private Charles J. Jelinek were wounded by enemy action. On the 10th of January another bridge was attacked and three Japanese soldiers were killed by Company A men. The same night, a lone Japanese soldier attempted to infiltrate into the Company A area and was promptly dealt with.

On the other hand, while in the Tambuco–Dolores area, Company C men somewhat evened the score by successfully dealing with enemy intruders and infiltrators with a box score of forty-

Running water to the company kitchens.

three Japanese soldiers killed and two taken prisoner. The Company suffered no casualties.

H&S and B Companies and Battalion Headquarters, during this time, remained on the beach at Ipil.

On the 15th of January, the entire Battalion moved by overland convoy and LSMs to Tarragona, a "rest camp" on the east side of Leyte. Lieutenants Otto W. Mourek and Allen K. Reid preceded the Battalion by a few days and located the new area for our camp and immediately began to improve it and to prepare it for the arrival of the Battalion. Upon arrival that evening, the men on the overland convoy began to set up the camp. The kitchens were prepared for the arrival of the LSMs. The bulk of the Battalion's personnel and tent areas were laid out. The LSMs arrived the following morning and the men were marched to the new area. Here they were greeted by the scene of pyramidal tents being erected. With everyone pitching in, a model camp appeared in a few days.

Kitchens were floored and screened in. The water section, supervised by Technical Sergeant Charles Williams, under the direction of Captain Robert K. Graham, dug a well, installed Navy ponton tanks atop a high coconut log tower, piped running water to the company kitchens, and erected and installed a huge shower. The men in the S-2 Section, supervised by Sergeant Carl A. Senal, under the direction of Captain Theodore C. Meinelt, cleared

Griffin's Lair—the most popular jungle theater on Leyte.

an area among tall coconut trees, painted white a twenty-by-twenty-foot canvas which was suspended between two towering palm trees, cut and dragged logs in for seats, and soon had "Griffin's Lair" the most popular jungle theatre on Leyte.

The rear echelon arrived from New Caledonia. Here at last was positive proof that the mythical New Caledonia was something real. Technician Fifth Grade John Belive assured everyone that it was so. Fresh vegetables, milk, Wacs, nurses—everything you have dreamed on those wet nights in a foxhole. He knew. While in charge of the equipment in the rear echelon he had sailed to New Caledonia from Hawaii, spent the summer, fall and most of the winter in this paradise of the Pacific and had then come on to the Philippines. In spite of the kidding he received about "some guys are always getting all the breaks," this 110-pound Griffin was glad to be back with the herd, and said so. Later he was awarded the Bronze Star medal for meritorious service.

The motion-picture machine was installed in the "Lair," and the men of the battalion, for the first time, began to enjoy a nightly movie, rain or shine—with very little shine. And packages, all our packages—Christmas gifts, magazines, newspapers from home—all that had been sent after we left Hawaii, began to

The new job was that of constructing ten coconut-log piers.

arrive. They were in sad condition. Technician Fifth Grade Henry P. Gawle, the eminent collector of pin-up girls, and battalion postman, opened shop. He sorted. Well, at least he divided. A number of packages were completely beyond use, but in the end many useful or tasty gifts from home were salvaged and many packages were in good shape. The men were joyful at the arrival of the parcels even though they were long overdue.

The job had arrived as soon as the Battalion had. There was always a job. The Battalion was still on the "24-hour basis." The men worked in three 8-hour shifts, and everything possible was done to give the men relaxation and to bring them entertainment between shifts. Natives were hired to do the camp cleaning. Again the Filipino women rendered good laundry service. A fellow could have a good shower, cold as the water was. PX supplies began to appear and beer arrived every two weeks.

It was then rumored that Technician Fifth Grade Harold Doan, keeper of Chief Warrant Officer George Lucas' supply records, between requisitioning shortages and consolidating reports was seen with a can of beer in hand. It was further rumored that if at any time there was beer in the vicinity, Doan got some of it. The Tarragona Camp was acclaimed by the men of the Battalion as the best setup they had had since Kahuku and the Hula dancers.

Private Gustave L. Hendricksen, known to everyone as "Hank," operated the movies. In this capacity he well proved his worth,

Mechanics began breaking open crates and assembling brand-new jeeps, trucks, cranes.

for through his dealings with Special Service, film libraries, and the Navy, it was not unusual for the Griffin's Lair to present not one, but even three features nightly. It was sometimes necessary for the men to sit patiently, huddled in the rain, while Hank paddled across the lagoon in a rubber boat to the unit on the other side and exchanged films. Even a few stage shows were presented for the men's entertainment. The Griffin's Lair was the most popular jungle theater on Leyte, showing on rainy nights to not less than a thousand GIs; when the weather was good two thousand or more would attend.

The new job was that of constructing ten coconut log piers on the beach at Tarragona for the purpose of unloading the new equipment that had started to arrive for the Division and attached troops, and to load it again when it came time for the next operation. There would be another operation. No one doubted that. The feeling was evident throughout the Battalion during the rest of January and the earlier part of February. Maybe it is a sixth sense that is possessed by a combat soldier which informs him it is time to muster his battle instincts. At any odds you chose, practically any one of the men would bet that the 233d was slated for another move.

Rumors floated: "I just heard from City Hall, we're going to Formosa."

"Just saw the Captain looking at a map of Japan, looks like Tokyo."

And there were the die-hards who insisted that, "We just got in a supply of brand new ODs and all of our medals and insignia; it's the States for sure."

Our new equipment was arriving. In the Motor Pool, mechanics began breaking open crates and assembling brand-new jeeps, trucks, cranes and bulldozers. This was a big moment for Captain Robert K. Graham's supply section. For once they could get almost anything the Battalion needed—and did. Technical Sergeant Clarence Carrol, the battalion supply sergeant, and his assistants, Staff Sergeant Fisher, Technicians Fifth Grade Harold Doan, Vernon Gibbard and John Belive, all under the watchful eye of Chief Warrant Officer George Lucas, began to dish it out. There were new items and replacement for worn articles. The supply men beamed when, after two operations without combat boots, they were able to issue them to the men. It would no longer be "leggins and liners" for the men of the 233d. With combat boots and the new engineers' caps the appearance of the Battalion took on a new glint.

Captain Christian C. Lutz, now Battalion operations officer, sent out the word to start constructing packing boxes and crates. Radios were given the once-over; switchboards were tightened up and inspected; machine guns zeroed in and oiled; old vehicles and equipment, not replaced, were given a coat of paint; and all of the many items to be taken along were given a final check-up and packed. Yes, the Battalion was going on another operation, but when? Where? These questions were foremost in everyone's mind.

The 25th of January is Battalion Day for the 233d Engineer Combat Battalion, commemorating the activation of the Battalion on that date in 1943. However, because of the pier job, the battalion commander postponed the celebration until the completion of the project. Thus, on the 22d of February, the Battalion celebrated Battalion Day for the first time.

The day was bright and clear. Griffin's Lair bristled with color. Flags, colors, the 77th Division Band, and the entire Battalion turned out. Major General Andrew D. Bruce, Commanding General of the 77th, was there to present the Bronze Star and the Purple Heart Medals to the men who had been awarded them

"To present the Bronze Star and the Purple Heart Medals to the men who had been awarded these decorations in the Guam and Leyte Campaigns."

in the Guam and Leyte Campaigns. Captain Theodore C. Meinelt gave a short history of the unit, and Lieutenant Colonel Orlan A. Johnson, then Major, and Colonel Cunningham, Commanding Officer of the 1118th Engineer Combat Group, addressed the Battalion. After the ceremonies the men were given the rest of the day off to participate in athletics, or maybe just to get some "flying time in" on their bunks. The night was celebrated with beer, six cans per man purchased from the unit funds, and Griffin's Lair presented a double-feature program, courtesy of Hank.

The morning of the 23d of February found the Battalion again assigned to the 307th Combat Team and preparing to load. The TQM team this time to load the cargo ship AKA 92, USS *Wyandot*, had already moved to the beach and was preparing plans and organizing the load. Lieutenants Victor E. Weaver and Allen K. Reid assisted by Technical Sergeant David H. Flanders, Technicians Fifth Grade Floyd K. Oglesby and Daniel M. Besaw, and Privates First Class Alfred W. Kruck, Jr., and George M. Kelly, made up the team. The loading was to be a "landing in reverse," and Companies A, B and C were assigned the task of shore party with the 1st, 2d, and 3d Battalions, respectively, of the 307th Combat Team. Navy Beach Parties were attached to the elements of the Battalion and moved into the Battalion area. Lieutenant Otto W. Mourek was placed in charge of the Battalion's heavier equipment, which was to be moved to the target area via LST convoy, and to precede the main convoy to a prearranged rendezous. An operational Command Post was established adjacent to the Regimental Command Post for coordinating the loading of supplies and equipment. Two control towers were erected for the Navy Beach Parties to enable them better to contact the control boat and to regulate small-boat activity on the beaches. Lighting units were installed so loading could continue through the night.

Actual shore-to-ship operations started on the 23d of February, with a ship's platoon and a shore platoon from Company B loading the 2d Battalion Landing Team's equipment and supplies aboard the USS *Eastland*. LCVPs and LCMs from the *Eastland* were used as lighterage. On the 25th of February the TQM Team commenced loading the USS *Wyandot*, using an infantry ship's platoon and a shore platoon from Company B. During the loading, which was in full swing by the 27th of February, all supply and equipment were handled by boats that were easily landed and retracted from the beach. From the 27th of February to the 7th of March the loading continued on a 24-hour basis, and on the 7th of March, the troops boarded their ships. In order to complete loading of the AKA 67, the USS *Suffolk*, Company A was ordered to remain on the beach, and on the 19th of March, having completed the loading, the company moved to the beach at Dulag and embarked on the USS *Mountrail*.

On the 15th and 16th of March the Battalion made two practice landings on selected beaches on the southern part of Leyte Gulf, with the troops of the 77th Division. The purpose of the landings was to synchronize the activity of the Battalion and the new Naval Beach Party. On the first landing the troops landed in LCVPs over a gradient beach of sandy coral. Beach panels, lateral telephones and ship-to-shore radio communications were set up. Unloading of cargo by the token method was simulated. On the 16th of March the troops landed over a rough coral-headed beach, necessitating the transfer of troops and cargo at sea from LCVPs to LVTs (water buffaloes). A beachhead was established for shore party operations.

Once again the 233d was going to war. This was to be their third major amphibious operation in nine months. Obviously some sort of record was being set, but again, whatever the job was to be the Battalion was going to do it well. This had become an obsession among the Griffins.

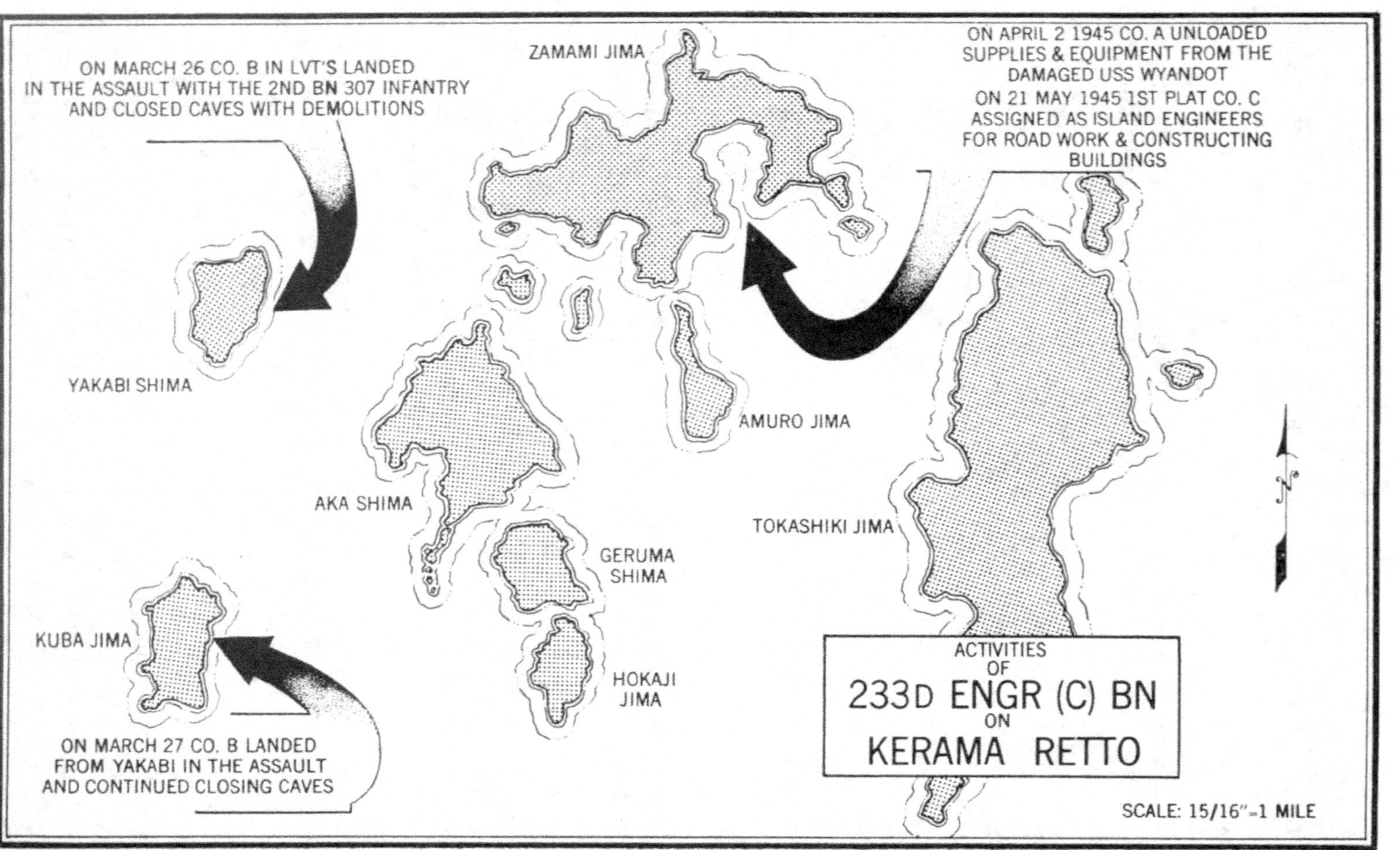

ON MARCH 26 CO. B IN LVT'S LANDED IN THE ASSAULT WITH THE 2ND BN 307 INFANTRY AND CLOSED CAVES WITH DEMOLITIONS
ON APRIL 2 1945 CO. A UNLOADED SUPPLIES & EQUIPMENT FROM THE DAMAGED USS WYANDOT
ON 21 MAY 1945 1ST PLAT CO. C ASSIGNED AS ISLAND ENGINEERS FOR ROAD WORK & CONSTRUCTING BUILDINGS
ZAMAMI JIMA
YAKABI SHIMA
AMURO JIMA
AKA SHIMA
TOKASHIKI JIMA
GERUMA SHIMA
HOKAJI JIMA
KUBA JIMA
ON MARCH 27 CO. B LANDED FROM YAKABI IN THE ASSAULT AND CONTINUED CLOSING CAVES
ACTIVITIES OF 233D ENGR (C) BN ON KERAMA RETTO
SCALE: 15/16"=1 MILE

CHAPTER XIII

THE JAP IN HIS OWN BACKYARD

The first operation the Griffins of the 233d had participated in, Guam, was completely free from the Japanese air force. The Rising Sun first appeared to us on the wings of a plane on the Ormoc Beachhead where it had caused some damage. When we learned we were going to sail right up to the middle of the chain of islands lying between Formosa and the Japanese home islands, just three hundred miles from the Imperial homeland itself, we knew that up to now we had merely been introduced to the Japanese air force. The air fighters from Japan would certainly be present this time in all their fury. It was true that the major portion of our Pacific Fleet was already operating in that vicinity, but here was the first convoy bearing a cargo of GI fighting men to enter those waters since the beginning of the war. Our destination was in the Okinawa Gunto, the eight islands of the Kerama Retto, fifteen miles west of Okinawa Shima, a mighty Japanese key point. We were preceding a bigger force that was to arrive a few days later; our only regret was that it wasn't the homeland itself, even Tokyo.

On the 21st of March, 1945 the convoy sailed from Leyte Gulf, the LST convoy having left two days before. On the second night out, the ship's loudspeaker called "General Quarters." This was not a dry-run; there were unidentified aircraft in the vicinity of the LST convoy up ahead. This was to continue every night from then on, but surprisingly there were no attempts made to attack either convoy. However, by daybreak the ships of the convoy and the escort craft were turning and twisting on their course dodging floating mines. When comparing notes about the trip with Lieutenant Mourek at a later date, it was discovered that the LST convoy did not sight any floating mines during the voyage. It then became obvious that the unidentified aircraft were Japanese bombers dropping floating mines in the path of the main convoy. This Japanese tactic proved unsuccessful because both convoys arrived at their destination undamaged. We did wonder, however, what the enemy would try next.

At 1400 on L day minus six Company B landed on Yakabi Shima, Kerama Retto, in assault with the 2d Battalion Landing

Team of the 307th Regimental Combat Team, 77th Infantry. The battalion commander accompanied Company B for directional purposes and for observation.

No enemy opposition was encountered and as very little re-supply was necessary the company, commanded by Captain Clarence E. Johnson, was given the mission of closing caves and destroying mining supplies as a protective measure against enemy reenforcements landing and occupying these positions. The island was secured the first day. In order to complete the demolition work, the company dug in and bivouacked overnight. A very few planes appeared the first day and were quickly taken care of by the destroyer screen. The following morning Company B, reinforced, with extra machine guns, moved from Yakabi Shima to Kuba Shima by LVTs. The accessible beaches were very short in width and narrow in depth. Inland the terrain rose steeply over rocky slopes. Again, there was no opposition from the enemy on the beaches and Company B spent its time closing caves and destroying enemy mining supplies with demolitions. The landing force dug in and remained on the island overnight, embarking on the USS *Eastland* the following morning.

During the six-day operations in the Kerama Retto there were numerous attempts to destroy our shipping by enemy air and suicide-boat attacks. Thus it became necessary for the convoy to pull out to sea every night and to return at daybreak. On the second night, when the convoy was returning to the target area, a lone Japanese plane dropped down out of a heavy cloudy overcast and dropped two bombs over the USS *Wyandot* which was carrying vehicles and supplies for the 307th Combat Team. Because of the large number of the Battalion's vehicles on this ship, an equal number of Battalion drivers were also aboard her as well as the Battalion TQM team and Captain Julius J. Simon, the battalion surgeon. The first bomb dropped into the water on the starboard side, aft, doing no harm to the ship. The second bomb dropped about fifteen feet to starboard, forward, exploding under water and causing a large rupture in the skin of the ship below the water line. The Number One and Two hold sections of the ship almost immediately filled with water and the ship began to sink.

The lone plane escaped back up into the cloud bank and the convoy continued on its way, leaving the then immobile ship floating around like a duck on a pond. One destroyer remained behind and circled the crippled ship, aboard which was plenty of

"Because of the pier job."

action. The landing craft were lowered into the water, One and Two hatches opened, and hose was dragged out. All hands turned to help. Aboard the ship was the heavy equipment operator, Sergeant Birdell B. Dunham. He remembered that the Battalion's fire trailer was on the top deck of Number Two hold. He immediately proceeded down into the hold and with the aid of other 233d men put the fire pumps into operation, pumping water out of the hold and over the side of the ship. This post he held voluntarily for the next forty-eight hours. The ship didn't sink, and finally, about fourteen hours later, partly on her own power and partly towed, she arrived in the harbor between the islands of the Kerama Retto. This harbor was soon to be called many names, by the Army and Navy men alike, such as "Death Valley," "Sick Bay," and "Davy Jones' Auxiliary Locker." Sergeant Dunham was later awarded the Bronze Star medal for his quick action and vigilance at the pumps. His efforts were markedly instrumental in preventing the ship from sinking.

On the fourth night of the operation the convoy moved out to sea to await further orders, the Kerama Retto having been secured, and to get out of the range of the ever-increasing Jap Kamikaze attacks However, while en route to the rendezvous area the convoy was attacked by eight Japanese suicide planes. Four ships were hit. Members of the Battalion were on two of those ships, the USS *Telfair*, carrying Company C, and the USS *Goodhue*. carrying Battalion Headquarters. The USS *Henrico*, used by Company A during maneuvers at Solomons Island, Maryland, was seriously damaged during that attack, and suffered many casualties. Fortunately the Battalion suffered no casualties during the attack. On the *Goodhue* the plane hit the aft mast, dropping its bombs over hold Number Five before sliding over the side into the sea.

The members of the Battalion aboard her were on the second deck down in hold Number Five. Sergeant Arthur B. Charbonnel, upon hearing the explosion rushed to the deck above and for many hours labored vigorously carrying wounded soldiers and sailors on his back down narrow ladders to the ship's sick bay. When he completed this job he worked in the sick bay helping the already exhausted medical aid men and pharmacist's mates to care for the many wounded men. For his work that night and his willingness to be of assistance to his comrades Sergeant Charbonnel was awarded the Bronze Star Medal.

The damaged ships were brought into the harbor at Kerama Retto where repair tugs were hard at work attempting to make them seaworthy again. The convoy proceeded out to sea to await further orders.

Things weren't quiet on Okinawa, however. The main force landed on Okinawa on the 1st of April, bringing on more Japanese air attacks. The attacks were constant now, almost day and night. Company A had been assigned the job of unloading from the landing craft on a little spit just off the Zamami Shima beach the damaged cargo from the *Wyandot*. It was necessary to unload immediately the water- and oil-soaked cargo from the holds of the ship to give the salvage crews access to the ruptured part of the vessel. During this unloading task, Company A was quartered aboard adjacent shipping. Their stay on any ship was of short duration, and after working on the beaches all day they usually returned, at nightfall, to a different ship.

The Battalion celebrated, for its first time, Battalion Day.

During the earlier part of the unloading, on a day when the ground swells were excessively high, Lieutenants Peter J. Langhans and Charles E. Schaub were both, at almost the same time, caught between the side of a ship and a landing craft, suffering serious leg and foot injuries. They were both evacuated to a hospital ship and thence to the States leaving Captain Richard S. Stevick and Lieutenant George Gray, Jr., as the only officers in Company A. The commanding officer of the battalion, Lieutenant Colonel Orlan A. Johnson, assigned Lieutenant Allen K. Reid to Company A and replaced him on the TQM team aboard the *Wyandot*, with Sergeant Carmen Muratore. Assuming an officer's duties, Sergeant Muratore handled his new assignment in a most efficient manner. Captured Korean laborers were helping Company A on the beach with the unloading, and upon the completion of the job Company A embarked on the USS *Goodhue* which was awaiting orders to join the convoy.

The convoy returned to Okinawa and dropped anchor in Hagushi Anchorage on the fourteenth day of the Okinawa Operation, the 14th of April, 1945. The USS *Goodhue* and the USS *Wyandot*, which were now repaired and seaworthy, arrived at the anchorage on the 15th of April. The Japanese air attacks were still continuing. The many ships in the anchorage were usually completely covered by a smokescreen. Suicide planes and suicide boats were active, and the men aboard were more than willing now to get ashore. Maybe it would be tough on the beach with sand and grit in your teeth, eyes and hair. Maybe the wind and weather would make leather out of your skin, but when a Japanese Kamikaze plane started at you, or one of those "Buzz Bombs" buzzed your way, you could at least dig in, and that's more than you could do on these steel decks. It's always that way with a land soldier when trouble comes at sea; he is lost and doesn't know what to do; there is no place to dig in on deck.

The next mission assigned the 77th Infantry Division was the capture and occupation of Ie Shima, an island off the western tip of Motobu Peninsula, Okinawa Shima, and one of the most important Japanese air bases in that sector. D-day for that operation was the 16th of April, 1945. This was one more step for the Griffins on their way to Japan.

CHAPTER XIV

INFANTRY AND ENGINEER TACTICS ON IE

LVTs sloshed ashore with their guns blazing on Beaches Red T-3 and Red T-4 at 1130 on the 17th of April, 1945. The place was Ie Shima. The defending Japanese soldier was reluctant to let us land, but land we did, the withering fire from the guns of the LVTs driving the Japs to cover. Along with the foot soldier of the 307th Infantry came the Griffins of the 233d. They felt the gravel of the beach crunch underfoot. They started forward, firing as they went. In another moment, one soldier was hurled high into the air. The gravel had exploded at his feet. Others were wounded by the blast.

"Mines!" someone yelled.

"Engineers!"

"Where are the Engineers?"

But the Engineers were already hard at it. The beach consisted of decomposed coral, forming a gravel-like surface extending inland for approximately forty feet. Sand dunes rose almost straight up for thirty feet. One dune ran parallel to the beach for the entire length of beaches Red T-3 and Red T-4. It was almost fifty feet wide on top, and the inland side sloped gently down for half a mile. It then rose gradually for the next half mile to the scrubs at the foot of the majestic lone mountain peak rising out of the island. The area between the sand dune and the scrubs at the edge of the hills, a mile wide, was flat and open, cultivated in places, the shrubs and trees necessary for concealment missing. At intervals, about one hundred yards apart, were breaks through the dunes, ideal for access roads inland. Mines blocked the passes through the dunes and were scattered over the beach area leading up to the breaks. The first mine located by the busy Griffins was made of wooden boxes containing picric acid with a mortar fuze detonator. Mine detectors proved useless in locating the hidden death-dealing boxes. There was one answer—probing. We did. We crawled on our hands and knees all over the beach, section by section, stabbing with trench knife, bayonet and stick.

Companies B and C and a Headquarters Detachment had landed. Company A with the 1st Battalion of the 307th Infantry

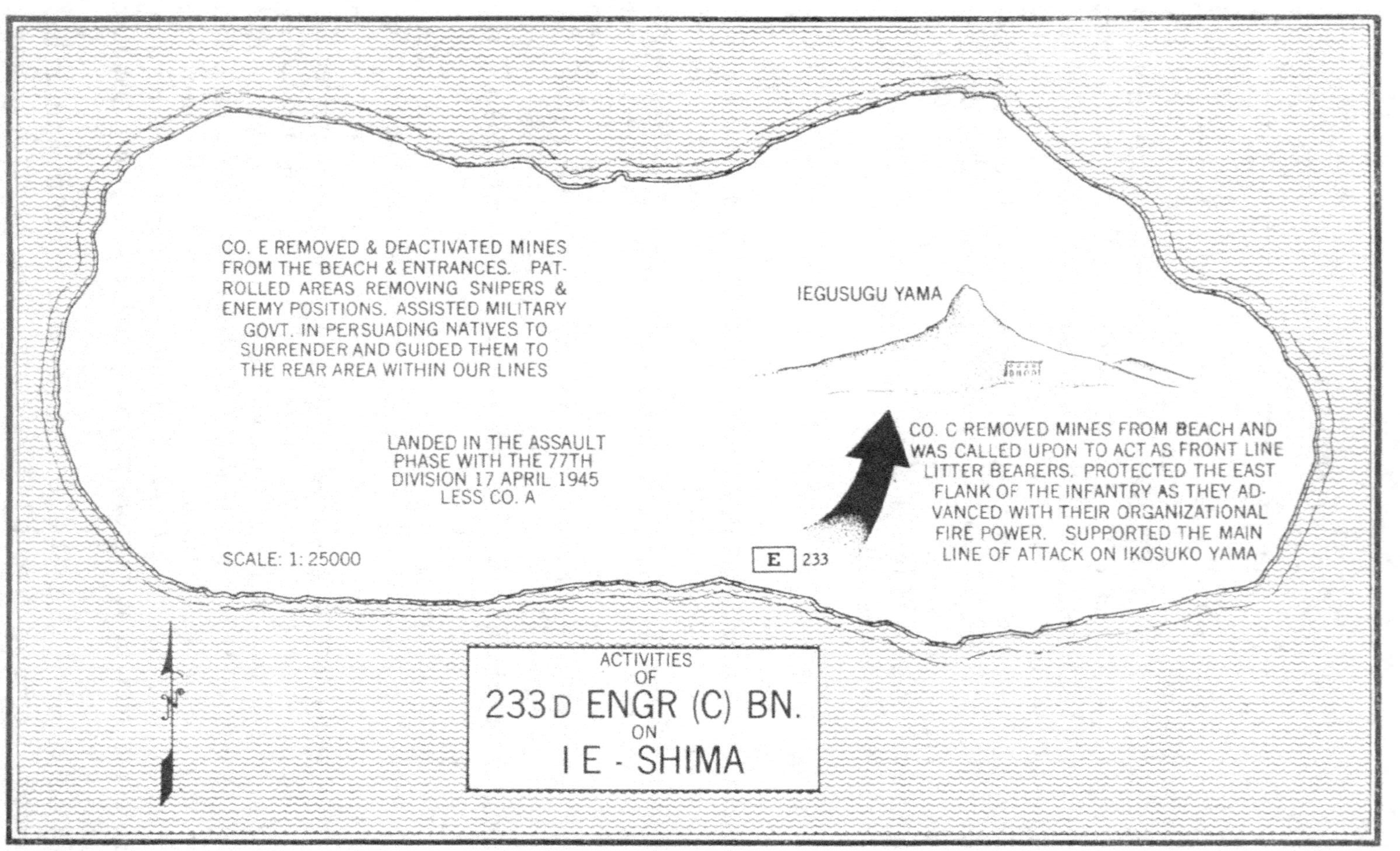

CO. E REMOVED & DEACTIVATED MINES
FROM THE BEACH & ENTRANCES. PAT-
ROLLED AREAS REMOVING SNIPERS &
ENEMY POSITIONS. ASSISTED MILITARY
GOVT. IN PERSUADING NATIVES TO
SURRENDER AND GUIDED THEM TO
THE REAR AREA WITHIN OUR LINES

IEGUSUGU YAMA

CO. C REMOVED MINES FROM BEACH AND
WAS CALLED UPON TO ACT AS FRONT LINE
LITTER BEARERS. PROTECTED THE EAST
FLANK OF THE INFANTRY AS THEY AD-
VANCED WITH THEIR ORGANIZATIONAL
FIRE POWER. SUPPORTED THE MAIN
LINE OF ATTACK ON IKOSUKO YAMA

LANDED IN THE ASSAULT
PHASE WITH THE 77TH
DIVISION 17 APRIL 1945
LESS CO. A

SCALE: 1: 25000

E   233

ACTIVITIES
OF
233D ENGR (C) BN.
ON
I E - SHIMA

was being held afloat by Tenth Army in strategic reserve. Hours passed; the crawling and probing continued. Mines were found and more mines removed and deactivated. The day's supplies were coming ashore. Food, ammunition, explosives, barbed wire, a jeep pulling a 37mm gun, another jeep being moved into the cleared section of the beach. Heavy fire came from the enemy. The men hugged the ground, crept behind the sand dunes. The infantry was moving inland, inching, dashing, firing. They crossed the open stretch, a mile across, reached the scrub growth on the other side—some of them.

The Navy evacuation station was set up at water's edge. The 233d medics assisted there. Casualties were arriving on the beach now, being dragged across the opening, over the dunes. The Navy sent them to the waiting hospital ship in LCVPs and LCMs. More casualties came. The assigned aid men could not keep up. The trip across the open flat space was slow and dangerous. Mortar fire, occasional snipers, and machine guns were the hazards. More litter bearers were needed at once. Company C got the job. Half of Company C joined the procession; running, dashing, crawling, dodging to get across the opening; then the long slow tedious trip back, dragging, carrying wounded men. The firing from the enemy seemed to increase. It seemed to be directed at the sweating, bleeding litter bearers, working in fours, getting wounded men out of the enemy fire to safety and care aboard the hospital ship.

The Griffins were in direct support of the infantry, fighting like infantry. The supplies were almost ashore. Minefields were being breached, and Company C men were braving the incessant fire from enemy dug-in up on the hill with a bird's-eye view of their every move. The enemy held the odds over these litter bearers, but they couldn't stop them.

The fire on the beach area had lessened considerably now. The infantry was driving the enemy back. Most of the fire was coming from flanking positions, some of which seemed to be right on the beach itself, among the sand dunes. Later, Warrant Officer Charles E. Kaylor, the battalion personnel officer, then acting Adjutant, said that each time he stuck his head out some one deliberately fired at it from close at hand. It was a day later when his personal antagonist was found in a hole beneath an oil drum cover.

Corporal Charles A. Warson, Company B, with his squad, was assigned the mission of clearing the beach areas of these snipers. His men spread out and began methodically covering every crack and cranny on the beach and in the dunes. Corporal Warson discovered a cave, concealed in the dune line. While cautiously investigating this cave, he became the target for several concussion charges thrown from the cave in rapid succession by Japanese soldiers inside. Though sustaining injuries from the exploding charges, he vigorously attacked the cave, alone, with hand grenades, killing one and seriously injuring the remaining enemy. For his courage in this action against the enemy, Corporal Charles A. Warson was awarded the Bronze Star Medal. He also received the Purple Heart for his wounds.

Inland to the left was a group of trees and low-growing bushes. From this direction came most of the firing that was hindering the beach and mine-removal operations. Lieutenant William W. Lassetter was sent with a patrol to clean out the enemy that had infiltrated back into this position. The patrol worked, under as much cover as could be found, around to the left flank and through a field to the rear of the tree group. They located and killed two Japanese soldiers in a cave, and their presence in the area held sniper fire from that vicinity to a minimum, and the work on the beach continued.

By 1430 the supplies were all ashore, and by 1530 all the mines had been removed from the beaches and access roads through the sand dunes. A total of one hundred and eighty mines was removed and deactivated by the Battalion during this period.

Inland, the infantry was gaining ground, but all automatic weapons available were needed on the front lines. The remainder of Company C, under the command of Captain John W. Petrie, Jr., then lieutenant, was assigned the mission of right-flank security for the 3d Battalion, 307th Infantry Regiment.

At 1830 heavy enemy mortar fire began again to fall along the beaches and on the access roads through the sand dunes. The elements of the Battalion, then in the beach area, were dug in on the perimeter and preparing to hold the line through the night. The night and the next morning brought numerous counter-attacks which were preceded by grenades, machine-gun fire, and mortar barrages, all directed at the beach area by the still stiffly-resisting Japanese soldiers.

On the morning of the 18th of April, 1945 the 233d was relieved of all beach responsibility by the 132d Engineers. Company C, under the command of Captain John W. Petrie, Jr., remained at its previously assigned missions of evacuating casualties from the front, flank security for the 3d Battalion, and security for the Regimental Command Post. Company B patrolled a proposed dump area inland from Red Beach T-4 to clear it of snipers and small groups of the enemy who still continued to harass personnel working on the beaches and dump sites. Two of the enemy were killed in a cave with hand grenades. Enemy mortar fire continued to fall in the area and heavy enemy sniper and machine-gun fire continued throughout the day. At 1400 Company C elements were relieved of their duties at the front lines and returned to the Battalion command post near the beach. Company B maintained guard on the beach and dumps during the night.

On the morning of the 19th, Company C resumed duties at the front with the 3d Battalion. Company B continued to maintain beach and dump guard and sent one platoon to relieve Company C men at the 307th Infantry Command Post.

During the afternoon Sergeant John M. McDaniel was acting as a litter bearer with three other men. He and these men made two trips under continuous enemy sniper, machine-gun and heavy mortar fire, with wounded from the front lines to the aid station. While carrying back a third wounded man an enemy mortar shell burst to the immediate rear of the litter team, killing the wounded man and seriously wounding three of the litter bearers. Sergeant McDaniel, though dazed by the explosion near him and still under concentrated enemy fire, with complete disregard for his personal safety dragged his three buddies into a nearby shallow ditch. He then covered the men with his own body, protecting them as best he could until the mortar barrage subsided. After administering first aid to each man, amid enemy sniper fire and machine-gun bursts, he, unaided, dragged each man over a crest and into a defile where they would be out of the line of direct enemy fire. He then continued to the beach aid station unarmed, as the blast of the mortars had destroyed or scattered the weapons. He procured an amphibious tractor and more help and they returned to evacuate the wounded men from the range of enemy mortar fire to the beach, to medical treatment and safety. For his gallantry in the face of the enemy and for his willingness to risk his own life to help his fellow soldiers, Sergeant John M. McDaniel was awarded the Silver Star Medal.

Sniper fire continued in the Battalion area and light mortar fire fell on Red Beach T-4. The predicted concentrated enemy banzai raid failed to materialize that night.

On the 20th of April Company C acted as infantry support to the 3d Battalion in their drive on the lone mountain peak, Iegusugu Yama, which began at 1000. Corporal Larry Tennity, affectionately known as "The Cub" by his teammates, was attached to Company C at the time. His duties here on the front lines as a combat soldier were far removed from his permanently assigned job as file clerk in the Adjutant's office. During the ensuing push, a heavily armed enemy strong point held up the advance of the line, and Corporal Tennity, with complete disregard for his own safety and purely on his own initiative, rose from his place of concealment, and in the face of the enemy fire, dashed across a clear field to a tank. The tank was buttoned up, and since the tank commander could not see or hear under the circumstances, had not noticed the strongpoint. Upon arrival at the tank Tennity pointed out the strongpoint to the tank commander and returned to his own place of concealment. The tank began firing .50-caliber machine guns at the enemy strongpoint. This fire was ineffective. Corporal Tennity, upon seeing this, again dashed over to the tank and suggested the tank commander fire his 75mm gun into the position. This done, the strongpoint was put out of commission and the troops continued their advance. Corporal Lawrence E. Tennity was awarded the Bronze Star Medal.

The platoon from Company B guarding the Regimental Command Post was given the mission of going over to the east side of the island to remove enemy civilians from a series of caves on that side. Over one hundred and fifty civilians were found in the caves. They were removed, and because of the enemy fire, the patrol took the civilians around the end of the island along the coast line and successfully brought them, without injury, to the stockade for prisoners of war on Red Beach T-2. Another platoon from Company B was closing enemy caves with demolitions, sealing inside the enemy soldiers who had been harassing our troops from these hideouts.

During the morning of the 21st of April Company C elements were relieved from the 3d Battalion and returned to the 233d area for rest and food. One platoon from Company B was sent to the front as litter bearers in place of Company C men. The other platoon from Company B commanded by Lieutenant William W. Lassetter, continued to blow up and seal numerous enemy caves containing snipers, mortar emplacements, machine guns, supplies, ammunition, arms and explosives.

On the afternoon of the 21st it became imperative that an enemy mortar crew, located in a cave on the approaches to Mount Iegusugu, be eliminated. Sergeant Duane D. Vegors, of Company B, leading a squad of six men, worked his way through heavy enemy fire to one of seven entrances to the cave. Assuming the initiative he gallantly advanced into the cave and brought out the mortar after throwing several hand grenades inside. The threat from the mortar fire now eliminated, Sergeant Vegors began bringing up explosives to seal the entrance to the cave. While he was placing a charge, a Japanese soldier attempted to escape from the cave. Sergeant Vegors, armed with only a pistol, boldly pursued the Jap and drove him into the open where men of the patrol quickly killed him. Again returning to his task, Sergeant Vegors continued setting his charges although he was frequently under heavy machine-gun fire. A sudden blast, set off inside the cave by the enemy, wounded Sergeant Vegors very seriously in the face, chest and arms. The leadership and gallantry displayed by Sergeant Vegors was instrumental in the accomplishment of the mission of closing the seven entrances to the cave, the capture of one enemy machine gun, one heavy mortar, and two knee mortars in addition to three known killed Japanese soldiers outside of the cave and the complete elimination of the uncounted number within. His actions were rewarded with the Silver Star Medal.

Ie Shima was secured on the 21st of April, 1945. It had been a vital Japanese air base, but like all the rest, the American fighting men had taken it. While this had been only a six-day struggle, the men of the 233d had seen some of their toughest fighting here. From the first they had been used with the infantry as infantry, but they had been lucky. One man had been killed and ten were wounded.

CHAPTER XV

THE 233D WORKS ON OKINAWA

At 0830 on the 22d of April the elements of the Battalion on Ie Shima boarded an LSM and landed on Okinawa on Orange Beach Number Two, coming ashore after dark on the same day. Company A had already landed on Orange Beach that afternoon. The ship's platoons and TQM team came ashore the following day, the 23d of April.

Upon landing on Okinawa, control of this Battalion passed from the 77th Infantry Division to operational control of Okinawa Island Command. The Battalion was given the primary mission of constructing various projects such as earthen causeways and land approaches for ponton causeways on Green Beaches; constructing third-class all-weather roads from beaches to dumps; operating coral pits and water points; clearing areas for malaria control; and constructing Class I, II, III, IV, and V dumps for the 7th Field Depot near Ishado on the east coast of the island.

Captain Eugene E. Skogerson had rejoined the Battalion and was now executive officer. Major Orlan A. Johnson, the battalion commander, was promoted to lieutenant colonel.

While the 7th Field Depot was being built, a forward command post comprising S-2, S-3, S-4 and assistant division engineer section personnel was operated near Ishado to direct that project. The remainder of headquarters was left with the Battalion at the base camp near Hiza. The camp was located about halfway between the two airports then being operated by the Marine Corps. Since these airports were the main object of the Japanese bombers, this put the Hiza camp right on the "milk-run." It was seldom that a night's sleep could be achieved by anyone. If it wasn't an enemy air raid in our immediate vicinity, it was a large Japanese artillery piece called the "ole man of the mountains," firing from the vicinity of Shuri Castle and lobbing shells at the southern airport. The singing wake of these shells and the explosions as they found an ammunition dump or a plane kept even the heaviest sleepers awake.

There was one new addition to the Battalion that was liked by one and all. Private First Class Delbert H. Sission, of Michi-

The 233d goes to work on Okinawa.

gan, had been promoted from water to ice. He, with the assistance of Private First Class Richard E. Varcoe, now operated the Battalion's ice machine, acquired just before leaving Leyte. The men of the Battalion will long remember the improvised ice cream that came from the ice machine under the operation of these two men, and they will long remember the long, odd hours of the day and night the two spent supplying ice and ice cream from then on. The cooling material was certainly a source of pleasure to every man in the Battalion and many members of adjacent units.

On the 3d of May the Battalion rear echelon arrived from Leyte, with the much-needed equipment that had been left behind. On the 5th of May, Company B, under the command of Captain Clarence E. Johnson, reinforced with men from H&S, A and C Companies, left for the 7th Field Depot job site. The bivouac area, water point, and dump areas were laid out, and the coral pit opened, and trucks began hauling coral to the bivouac and dump areas. Several times work was slowed down by the incessant rains, but work continued on a 24-hour basis. By the 9th of May the class II, III, and IV dump areas were too wet for construction to continue, but clearance of the class V dump continued. Reconnaissance for the new coral pit was made. On the 12th of May the gravel pit was opened, and sand was hauled into the Class I, II and IV dumps. Trees and walls were cleared, using demolitions to blast them out; in the Class III dump, slot Num-

The Battalion began operations on a coral pit.

ber Six had already been laid out. Work continued throughout the week. Roads were built, culverts installed in all dump areas, and new roads were surveyed. By the 26th of May, with work almost completed, the Headquarters personnel were ordered back to the base camp at Hiza. The Battalion was to be relieved from attachment to the 1st Engineer Special Brigade and the Third Amphibious Corps.

On the 1st of June the Battalion was attached to the 1165th Engineer Combat Group for operational purposes only. Company A was assigned the job of placing coral on the road to the III Amphibious Corps Hospital area, and Company C began work on the maintenance of the Class III reserve dump roads between forks of the Bisha Gawa. A general area for the 381st Station Hospital was laid out by battalion surveyors. The Battalion began operation of a coral pit on Route One, north, near Yontan Airfield, while steady rains hampered all jobs. A sanitation and malaria control job was started by members of Company A, under the supervision of Lieutenant Allen K. Reid, necessitating the burning of huts lining the highways, but on the 4th of June all work was brought to a standstill because of rains and high winds.

A typhoon was expected that night at nine o'clock. The winds, accompanied by driving rains, blew throughout the night; however, daylight brought a clear day and work was resumed. Company A was assigned the job of assembling Quonset huts for a radio

Company A, on the first of July, was assigned the job of leveling and grading.

intercept station. On the 10th of June a new coral pit began operation with Sergeant Carmen Muratore supervising the work.

The danger on a considerable part of the island from enemy air attacks was not due to the attacking planes, as they concentrated on the major installations such as airports and unloading beaches, where the tons and tons of supplies necessary to keep the large number of forces on Okinawa on the go were stored. Most of the danger was from the rain of fragments from our own antiaircraft bursts. Since the numerous nightly blackouts were greatly hindering construction on the island, the engineers were ordered to continue on their jobs during a flash red unless the attacking planes were right overhead and the antiaircraft bursts were breaking overhead. That was the way it went, job after job, air raid after air raid, day after day and night after night. The accomplishments of the Battalion were a very small part of the huge accomplishments of the Army on Okinawa. Small as their part seemed they knew it was all a part of a giant strategic move. Okinawa was to be the jumping-off place for future attacks against the Japanese Empire, and a resupply base for the next operation—their operation. No one doubted that they would once again move closer to the homeland. Perhaps the next move would be Japan itself.

On the 14th of June the Battalion was alerted for movement from the island with the 77th Infantry Division to a rest and rehabilitation center. All work was completed, and equipment, drawn especially for the jobs, was being turned in preparatory to the move. Company B returned to base camp, and preparations for the move were completed. On the 19th of June the Bat-

And with proper ceremony, Company A launched its second barge.

talion was relieved of all work orders by the 1165 Engineer Group, and then reverted to control of the 77th Division—assigned the job of loading out the Division. After four different changes of orders within the next two days, the Battalion was finally notified that it would not leave with the 77th Division, but instead move to the Naha area.

On the 22d of June an advance party was sent to Naha to locate the new bivouac area. The orders to load out the division were rescinded and preparations were then made for the move to Naha.

The new bivouac area in Naha was located on Ono Yama, a little island in the center of the Kokuba River which ran through Naha on its way to the harbor. On the 26th of June the remainder of the Battalion arrived and proceeded to level off the area and construct camp. Mess halls were constructed (Company A's with a tile roof), a theater was set up, PX installed, and electric lights supplied for each pyramidal tent. The Battalion was then assigned to the 1497th Engineer Port Construction and Repair Group for operational purposes.

Company A, on the 1st of July, was assigned the job of leveling and grading the dump areas at the Medical Corps Depot, the Corps of Engineers Depot, salvaging existing buildings, and hauling away rubble. Company B was assigned the construction of one mile of a two-lane, all-weather road, and Company C, the construction of a Bailey Bridge at the Ordnance Service Center and the leveling and grading of a dump area at the Ordnance Depot in Naha. On the 3d of July, because of shortage of equipment, Company A's work on the Engineer Depot was suspended.

Coral hauled and roads topped.

On the 5th of July Lieutenant Henry A. Lind reported from the Kerama Retto Garrison Force Headquarters to the battalion commander that his platoon was no longer doing engineering work, but only supervisory work over the natives hand-grading the roads on the island. Lieutenant Lind and his platoon had been assigned to do engineering work on the island of Zamami for the past month. During this period they had assisted the antiaircraft units by digging in their gun emplacements, maintained the roads, and built a Cub-plane strip. Lieutenant Lind had been assigned as Island Engineer and was in charge of all engineering work in the Kerama Retto.

The 7th of July found Company A relieved from all other jobs, and assigned the task of assembling approximately eight hundred tons of sectional steel barges at the quayside, in Naha Port. Work on the Medical Depot was then assigned to Company B for completion, and to Company C went the job of completing the Engineer Depot. On the 12th of July, and with proper ceremony, Company A launched its second barge from the ways at the Naha Port. The next day Company B was assigned to the pleasant task of salvaging the Naha Saki Distillery, the job consisting of removing all usable pipe, valves, fittings and tanks, and delivering them to the Engineer Depot. The ensuing weeks, like the past, were periods of ceaseless effort on the part of every man in the Battalion. Roads were continuously maintained by all companies, all through the entire Naha Port Area. Warehouses were built, dumps cleared, fences and barges built, coral hauled

A three-level loading pit.

and roads topped. Work for the 233d was still on a "24-hour basis."

A mammoth new coral pit had been established by the Battalion north of Naha. Captain Roland D. Vandale was in charge of operations. Sergeants Carmen A. Muratore and David Flanders were his assistants. A large proportion of all the coral used in the Naha and adjacent areas came from this huge pit. It was developed into a three-level loading pit, and strings of trucks constantly drove to and from the big shovels which heaped them high with coral. As with all other battalion projects, the coral pit operated around the clock, stopping only to change shovel operators. On Okinawa the 233d had dropped the "Combat" and retained the "Engineer." They were now construction engineers on what was fast becoming the strongest and largest Army base in the West Pacific. Everyone knew, though, that the next step for the Griffins would be Japan and more combat. Much more combat.

CHAPTER XVI

WE LOOK TOWARD HOME

Some changes had taken place in the 233d in the past months. Major William D. Long and Lieutenants Max L. Daley and Frederick W. Bloomfield had been evacuated during the Leyte Campaign. Eugene E. Skogerson, then a captain, replaced Major Long as executive officer of the Battalion, prior to our leaving Leyte. Lieutenants Clarence J. Wangrin and Frank A. Vajda arrived shortly after our arrival on Okinawa. Now, during the latter part of our stay at Naha, more changes were taking place. Captain Richard S. Stevick, who had been the battalion's operation officer during the Guam campaign and later commanded Company A in a very successful manner through the Leyte and Ryukyu campaigns, was evacuated to a Hospital on Guam for eye treatment. The men and officers of the Battalion were going to miss Captain Stevick. He had been a real leader, well liked by the men of his command, and a good engineer. Lieutenant Harley T. Crawford was assigned as commanding officer of Company A, in his place.

A few days later another noticeable change came. Captain Nicholas C. Angel, commanding officer of H&S Company throughout all three campaigns, was evacuated to the States and hospitalized. Better known as "Nick," Captain Angel had served well. He had exemplified an affection for the men of his command seldom equaled. Nick was going to be missed also. Lieutenant Byron C. Hanson was assigned the command of H&S Company. Both Captain Stevick and Captain Angel had been awarded the Bronze Star Medal.

The next change, coming in quick succession, was the transfer of Captain Julius J. Simon, the Battalion Surgeon, to a hospital unit. Captain Simon had been the life of the party in more ways than one. He knew as much about each man as the man himself. He had looked down the men's throats, felt their pulses, fixed them up when they were injured, treated them when they were sick, and put the needle to them many more times than the men could really welcome. He was certainly going to be missed. The Battalion, however, was glad to welcome Captain Benjamin F. Levey, Jr., as the battalion surgeon. It was also about this time that

"In the past, as long as they received their pay . . . "

Lieutenants Robert E. Jackson, Eugene P. Meyers, and Jack O. Lynch joined the Battalion's ranks.

The War Department had inaugurated the "point system." This got you home, so they said—but when? This now familiar question, "When do I go home?" was also the reason that WOJG Charles E. Kaylor became the man of the hour. It was the duty of the battalion personnel officer to compute the points for each man and to keep liaison with higher headquarters to get the orders. It appeared that the men thought that it was up to Mr. Kaylor to get the transport tickets, maybe even airplane tickets, for each man, and tell them when to leave. In the past as long as they eventually received their pay, and their allotments got to the folks at home, and their insurance was in order, the men had accepted Mr. Kaylor as merely another officer in headquarters, but now:

"Let's go see Mr. Kaylor. Let's find out when he is going to send us home."

"You don't suppose the C.O. would make him keep us here, do you?" And so it went, day after day. Long before coming over-

The next day things went as usual.

seas, and throughout the campaigns, Mr. Kaylor and his section, Technical Sergeant Linus G. Becker, Technician Fourth Grade John J. Foster, and Corporals Ronald J. Rooney of Company A, Jimmy Z. Ortiz of Company B, Adolph J. Rosol of Company C and Joseph A. Vermette of H&S Company, had been keeping the records of each man and officer in the Battalion. The work of these men is tremendously important. It must be extremely accurate. Then when the shooting is over they are never mentioned. They receive no credit, except that they themselves know that, like all the other Griffins, they have done their jobs well. However, with the point system they came into their own. They became well known to every man in the Battalion. They were followed, questioned—these were the men who would get us home.

On the 16th of August word came of the atom bomb and the Japanese surrender offer, and the entire island was the scene of wild rejoicing. Searchlights and tracers crisscrossed the sky, flares and rockets were fired; everyone thought that the war was over. The next day things went on as usual, and five days later, when the official word came through, not a shot was fired.

Now more than ever, the main thing in everyone's mind was the point system. Mr. Kaylor, upon returning from an official visit to higher headquarters, would be met at the gate to the battalion area by high-point men. He had to hide out when he

All hell broke loose.

was in the battalion area, to get his work done. The old Army man, Leroy Gager, one hundred and fourteen points, would catch anyone he could find, sit him down and proceed to tell him what was wrong with the Battalion, the Division, the Army, and the point system, while Sergeant "Sack" Baker of Company A, also in the "old Army man" bracket, and with points running into three figures, sat by himself in the corner, mumbling to no one, with a faraway look in his eye. For the rest, or most of the rest, those sixty or seventy points didn't look too high, and they didn't care much for the point system.

On the 27th of September Mr. Kaylor finally returned with the first orders. Things happened and about eighty men moved out for home. From that day on the Battalion began growing steadily smaller. From eighty-five it dropped to eighty. Another group left.

In the middle of everything, on the 9th of October hell broke loose on the island of Okinawa. Winds coming from the north, south, east and west, all converged on the tiny island to form a

Winds came from the north, south, east, and west.

typhoon. The focal point of the entire blast, lasting about thirty hours, seemed to lie in the center of the battalion area. After the first big blast, when half the tents in the area came down, the men began to sit up and take notice. Everybody was running around frantically trying to find stakes, ropes, poles, rocks— anything to buck the force of the wind. But whoever was doing the blowing smiled at mortal man's pitiful efforts, even though the men were engineers, and proceeded to blow everything down except Company A's mess hall. That was the center of refuge, the only place where the men could get out of the wind, wet, and cold, and possibly get some sleep. That no one was hurt seemed a miracle. With all the tents, tent floors, bags, poles, and what-have-you spinning through the air, it seemed that someone would be sent flying galley west, but everybody stayed on the ground.

The points progressively dropped from eighty to seventy-six, with the 38-year-old men also leaving. Finally after much prep-

A typhoon.

aration and cancellation of orders the Battalion, or what was left of it, boarded LST 687, on the 7th of November, 1945. The Battalion was now relieved of all other assignments and attachments and assigned to the Sixth Army.

On the 12th of November they landed in the town of Kure, the main Japanese naval base, on Honshu Island. Here, at long last, amid rubble and wreckage, were paved streets, street cars, charcoal-burning buses, stores, shops, a local playhouse, an abundance of souvenirs—in short, a city. The Griffins had traveled the long road to Japan.

Upon arrival, all men with seventy-one points or above, and all officers with ninety points or above, were alerted to leave for home on the 14th of November. This took half of the remaining personnel, including the commanding officer of the 233d, Lieutenant Colonel Orlan A. Johnson. Colonel Johnson had come to the Battalion two days before it left Camp Pickett for overseas, as executive officer. On Hawaii, while a major, he took command of the Battalion. He had, since then, led the Griffins over the reef at Guam, and through the hardships and mud of that campaign; again onto the beach, near Desposito on Leyte, and

Proceeded to blow everything down except Company A's messhall.

throughout the Ormoc campaign; later he went ashore on the Kerama Retto with Company B; directed and assisted the men of the Battalion on Ie Shima. On Okinawa he had sponsored a party for the noncommissioned officers of the Battalion, stating that he wished it could have been for all the men. Now, with his orders relieving him of his command and returning him to civilian status, the men looked back over that long hazardous road to Japan. They remembered a commanding officer firm in his convictions, precise in his decisions; they had obeyed without question, and he had guided them through their many noteworthy accomplishments. He had led them through to Japan. The remaining men and officers, even with the war over and their sole task to wait for their turn to start homeward, would certainly miss their commanding officer.

Captain Robert K. Graham assumed command of the Battalion. Everything not necessary in living from day to day was turned in. Convoys were arranged for the one hundred and seventy men left in the Battalion, taking them on a tour through Hiroshima where they could view the destruction created by one lone atomic bomb. What the men saw, even after they saw it, was unbelievable. These men were accustomed to seeing death and destruction daily, but this by one bomb—it didn't seem possible.

One member of the Battalion remarked, "Everyone in the world should see this."

Another answered, "If they could, there would be no more wars. Men like us wouldn't have to be away from home, fighting, sacrificing and dying for what is right."

The next few days found Captain Benjamin F. Levey and Lieutenants Jack O. Lynch, Eugene P. Myers, Frank A. Vajda and Clarence J. Wangerin transferred to other units at Kure; they had arrived overseas during the Okinawa campaign. Their points didn't warrant their going home just yet. The men and officers continued to leave during the next few weeks as the points dropped two or three numbers every two or three days or so, until Lieutenant Allen K. Reid remained alone with the records. He was the 233d Engineers. By early January he was on his way to the States. The 233d Engineer Combat Battalion was inactivated.

CHAPTER XVII

IN CONCLUSION

The 233d Engineer Combat Battalion has been to war. It has heaped accomplishment upon accomplishment. The Battalion has lived, and its members do not want it to die. With this thought in mind, and to enable the members of the Battalion to get together from time to time and talk things over after the war, an association was formed—the 233d Combat Battalion Association—on Okinawa during the latter days of the Battalion's stay on that island. From the enlisted ranks, the following officers were elected: Sheldon J. Shalett, President; John H. Foster, Chairman of the Board; John A. Bickford, Secretary-Treasurer; Ronald J. Rooney and David L. Snow, board members. The office of the association is at 5144 Cornell Avenue, Chicago, Illinois. Members may contact the association officers at that address. Board meetings, the publishing of the History, and planning for a first convention will be conducted with the Headquarters as a base of operations.

In the writing of this History of the 233d Engineer Combat Battalion, I have found great pleasure in assembling and recording the material that has gone to make up this book. In reviewing the actions of the Griffins when facing the enemy on the battlefield, while again and again displaying the never-failing will to do the job well at any cost, the thought has come to me that the men and officers will carry back into civilian life that same will that carried them through the accomplishment of their every mission in the Pacific. Whatever the job, for the good of our country, we can do it and do it well. To those gallant comrades we left behind on the field of battle, for these men and officers of the 233d Engineer Combat Battalion I say,

"Thanks, Fellows, may God be with you until we meet again."

Victor E. Weaver

March 1, 1946
Washington, D. C.

PART TWO
THE STATISTICS

1. CHRONOLOGY

1943	January	25	Activation of the 233d Engineer Combat Battalion
	March	1	Arrival of first group of recruits
	June	6	End of basic training . . . "Graduation"
	July	14	North Carolina Maneuvers
	September	13	Move to Camp Pickett—Birchin Lake
	October	15	Move to Fort Pierce N.A.T.B.
	November	24	Return to Camp Pickett—Tent City
	November	28	Alerted for overseas movement
	December	28	Solomons Island Maneuvers—defensive
1944	January	3	End of Defense Phase
	January	20	Solomons Island Maneuvers—offensive
	February	2	Return to Camp Pickett
	March	4	Death of Lieutenant Colonel Gates
	March	6	Lieutenant Colonal Jurvic assumes command
	March	8	Movement to Fort Lawton, Seattle P.O.E.
	March	21	Departure from the United States
	March	28	Arrival at Oahu, T.H.
	May	3	Major Johnson assumes command
	July	9	Departure for Guam
	July	22	Arrival at Guam
	August	12	Guam secured
	November	2	Departure from Guam
	November	23	Arrival at Leyte, P.I.
	December	7	Assault landing with the 77th Division at Desposito, Ormoc Bay
	December	8	Ipil Beach set in operation
	December	25	Move to front lines at Dipi
1945	January	1	Move to Dolores by Companies A and C
	January	15	Battalion moves to Tarragona
	January	25	Battalion Day
	February	22	Battalion Day Ceremonies
	March	7	Departure from Leyte
	March	26	Landings in Kerama Retto
	April	16	Landings on Ie Shima
	April	22	Landing on Okinawa
	June	26	Move to Naha
	September	2	VJ Day
	November	7	Departure for Japan
	November	12	Debarkation at Kure, Honsho Island, Japan Inactivation

2. BATTLE CASUALTIES

KEY—KIA: Killed in action.
     LWA: Lightly wounded in action.
     SWA: Severely wounded in action.
     LIA: Lightly injured in action.

Saturnino M. Ramos, Pfc.   38216134
  LWA—21 July, 44; Guam, M. I., accidental discharge of gun, gunshot wound, right hand.

Albert E. Anderson, Pfc.   36629920
  LWA—5 Aug., 44; Guam, M. I.

Harry A. Johnson, Jr., Pvt.   36455202
  KIA—12 Aug., 44; Guam M. I., Jap sniper.

James F. Slattery, Jr., Pfc.   11085744
  LWA—21 Aug., 44; Guam, M. I., sniper fire, penetrating wounds, right shoulder.

Harry E. McDaniel, S. Sgt.   32383472
  KIA—6 Dec., 44; Leyte, P. I., paratrooper attack.

Gilbert T. Owens, Pvt.   37454492
  SWA—6 Dec., 44; Leyte, P. I., paratrooper attack, penetrating wounds, head and stomach.

Oscar A. Coleman, Pvt.   38487687
  SWA—6 Dec., 44; Leyte, P. I., paratrooper attack, penetrating wounds, head and face.

John J. Downes, Pfc.   36510466
  LWA—6 Dec., 44; Leyte, P. I., paratrooper attack, multi-superficial wounds, back and right thigh.

Robert A. St. Mary, Pvt.   36571023
  LWA—6 Dec., 44; Leyte, P. I., paratrooper attack, penetrating wound, left elbow.

Francis F. Walker, Tech. 4   37508540
  LWA—7 Dec., 44; Leyte, P. I., lacerating wounds, third finger, right hand.

David J. Rapp, Pfc.   36190294
  LWA—8 Dec., 44; Leyte, P. I., penetrating wound, groin.

Leopoldo Lopez, Pfc.   38348099
  SWA—9 Dec., 44; Leyte, P. I., gunshot wound, right arm.

Richard H. Forbes, Pvt.   36739308
  KIA—10 Dec., 44; Leyte, P. I., bombing raid.

Harold J. Kipfmiller, Tech. 4
  KIA—Leyte, P. I.

Bernice W. Vest, S. Sgt.   33210087
  SWA—13 Dec., 44; Leyte, P. I., accidental discharge of gun, gunshot wounds, right leg.

Victor Swenders, Tech. 5   36577130
  LIA—15 Dec., 44; Leyte, P. I., fracture of right shoulder.
Robert L. Greene, Pfc.   35514104
  LWA—15 Dec., 44; Leyte, P. I.
Warren Lauer, Pvt.   36647009
  SWA—18 Dec., 44; Leyte, P. I., bombing raid, FCCR and shoulder,
    multi-laceration wounds, back and head.
Rolla Browning, Pvt.   39331429
  SWA—18 Dec., 44; Leyte, P. I., bombing raid, penetrating wounds, back
    and right thigh.
Waldo R. Nickel, Tech. 4   37266316
  SWA—18 Dec., 44; Leyte, P. I., bombing raid, penetrating wounds, face
    and left arm.
Joe J. Masten, Pvt.   32674998
  SWA—18 Dec., 44; Leyte, P. I., bombing raid, penetrating wounds, chest.
Oliver H. Bushman, Cpl.   36809020
  LWA—18 Dec., 44; Leyte, P. I., bombing raid, shell fragment in right
    hand.
Anthony L. Cocuzzo, Tech. 5   31157770
  KIA—18 Dec., 44; Leyte, P. I., bombing raid.
Josiah H. Curtis, Sgt.   37216250
  LWA—18 Dec., 44; Leyte, P. I.
Herman Monroe, Sgt.   36185355
  LWA—18 Dec., 44; Leyte, P. I.
Frank E. Ciesielski, Pvt.   36577376
  LWA—18 Dec., 44; Leyte, P. I.
Edward J. Williams, Cpl.   31341685
  LWA—18 Dec., 44; Leyte, P. I.
Lloyd W. Shellenbarger, Pvt.   36577313
  KIA—21 Dec., 44; Leyte, P. I., killed by enemy patrol while on bridge
    guard.
Michael J. Rawlings, Sgt.   37332800
  KIA—21 Dec., 44; Leyte, P. I., killed by enemy patrol while on bridge
    guard.
Robert Goulet, Pvt.   36809197
  SWA—21 Dec., 44; Leyte, P. I., while on bridge guard, severe lacerating
    wounds, chest and right leg
William B. Ide, Jr., Pfc.   37508412
  SWA—21 Dec., 44; Leyte, P. I., while on bridge guard, penetrating
    wounds, chest, legs, and face.
Ralph Marzucca, Tech. 4.   31251025
  LWA—27 Dec., 44; Leyte, P. I., multi-wound, upper lip, wrist, and elbow.
Richard S. Stevick, Capt.   O-1106507
  LIA—8 Jan., 45; Leyte, P. I., lacerating wounds, face and head.

Roy A. Killam, Tech. 5   37215163
  KIA—8 Jan., 45; Leyte, P. I.
Jesse D. Guyer, Tech. 5.   17088082
  LWA—8 Jan., 45; Leyte, P. I., gunshot wound, right leg.
LeRoy G. Reason, Sgt.   37425713
  LWA—8 Jan., 45; Leyte, P. I.
Charles J. Jelinek, Pvt.   36649004
  LWA—8 Jan., 45; Leyte, P. I.
Robert D. Walther, Sgt.   37426082
  SWA—11 Jan., 45; Leyte, P. I., sniper fire, penetrating gunshot wounds,
    head and face.
John P. Raffa, Pfc.   32666220
  LIA—2 Apr., 45; aboard U.S.S. Telfair.
Kenneth R. Armstrong, Pfc.   36455322
  SWA—17 Apr., 45; Ie Shima, R. I.
Harley T. Crawford, 1st Lt.   O-1111002
  LWA—17 Apr., 45; Ie Shima, R. I.
Christian C. Lutz, Capt.   O-1105633
  LWA—17 Apr., 45; Ie Shima, R. I.
Louis S. Bozin, Pfc.   35023972
  LWA—17 Apr., 45; Ie Shima, R. I., penetrating wound, right leg.
Gerald L. Koch, S. Sgt.   37454483
  LWA—20 Apr., 45; Ie Shima, R. I.
Stanley C. Hahula, Sgt.   36518230
  SWA—20 Apr., 45; Ie Shima, R. I., litter bearer, severe lacerating wound,
    right leg.
Joseph H. Sokola, Tech. 4.   36516716
  SWA—20 Apr., 45; Ie Shima, R. I., litter bearer, penetrating wounds,
    right leg.
Charles L. Nehrbass, Pvt.   39397410
  SWA—20 Apr., 45; Ie Shima, R. I., caused by blast, penetrating wounds.
Wayne S. Deal, Tech. 5.   37332827
  LWA—20 Apr., 45; Okinawa, R. I., AA fire, penetrating wounds, back.
Domenic J. Pitrone, Sgt.   36186031
  LWA—20 Apr., 45; Okinawa, R. I., AA fire, penetrating wounds, back.
Robert L. Scheibl, Pfc.   36646206
  LWA—20 Apr., 45; Okinawa, R. I., AA fire.
Gordon R. Wood, Pfc.   37603480
  SWA—21 Apr., 45; Ie Shima, R. I., caused by blast, penetrating wounds,
    face and chest.
Duane D. Vegors, Sgt.   37425489
  SWA—21 Apr., 45; Ie Shima, R. I., penetrating wounds, extensive.
Daniel V. Bostrom, Cpl.   37332765
  SWA—21 Apr., 45; Ie Shima, R. I.

Charles A. Warson, Cpl. 36574575
  LWA—21 Apr., 45; Ie Shima, R. I.
Theodore P. Hagstrom, Pfc. 32382719
  KIA—21 Apr., 45; Ie Shima, R. I.
Emil H. Wildauer, Pfc. 36577301
  SWA—21 Apr., 45; Ie Shima, R. I.
George W. Armstrong, S. Sgt. 36517875
  SWA—19 May, 45; Okinawa, R. I., penetrating wounds.
Robert F. Pooler, S. Sgt. 32384443
  SWA—19 May, 45; Okinawa, R. I.
Victor Mark, Sgt. 36518094
  SWA—19 May, 45; Okinawa, R. I.
William F. Regan, Jr., Sgt. 11065865
  SWA—19 May, 45; Okinawa, R. I.
Kenneth W. Cramton, Cpl. 36575636
  SWA—19 May, 45; Okinawa, R. I.
Patrick H. Donahue, Cpl. 37509068
  KIA—19 May, 45; Okinawa, R. I.
Ellsworth D. Pool, Pfc. 37662513
  SWA—19 May, 45; Okinawa, R. I.
Jerome J. Barnett, Tech. 5. 36518297
  KIA—19 May, 45; Okinawa, R. I.
Joseph J. Tarasewicz, Sgt. 36809305
  SWA—27 July, 45; Okinawa, R. I., perforating wound, right foot.

3. AWARDS
SILVER STAR (GALLANTRY IN ACTION)
BRONZE STAR (HEROIC ACHIEVEMENT)

Name	Rank	Company	Award
McDaniel, John M.	Sgt.	C	Silver Star
Vegors, Duane D.	Sgt.	B	Silver Star
Ide, William B., Jr.	Pfc.	C	Silver Star
Warson, Charles A.	Sgt.	B	Bronze Star
Tennity, Lawrence E.	T/5	H&S	Bronze Star
Sievers, Floyd R.	Pfc.	C	Bronze Star
Johnson, Wallace M.	T/4	Med. Det.	Bronze Star
Ruesch, Rondo W.	1st Lt.	H&S	Bronze Star
Green, Howard J.	T/4	B	Bronze Star
Goulet, Robert	Pfc.	C	Bronze Star
Crawford, Harley T.	1st Lt.	A	Bronze Star

BRONZE STAR (MERITORIOUS SERVICE)

Name	Rank	Company
Guam 21 July, 44–10 August, 44:		
Olaf H. Johanson	T/4	A
Francis G. Peters	Sgt.	A
Francis H. McGowan	T/5	C
Harlan L. Dicks	S. Sgt.	C
Ralph C. LaPorte	S. Sgt.	A
Harold C. Frost	T/4	A
John W. Petre	Capt.	C
Victor L. Smith	S. Sgt.	A
Harlan W. Middlemiss	Cpl.	A
Julius J. Simon	Capt.	Med.
David Hom	T/4	Med.
Kenneth H. Hovdeness	Pfc.	H&S
Verne G. Erickson	T/4	H&S
Bernice W. Vest	S. Sgt.	Med.
Charles C. Herb	Sgt.	A
Nicholas C. Angel	Capt.	H&S
Robert F. Brelsford	S. Sgt.	B
Leyte 20 October, 44–25 December, 44:		
George W. Armstrong	S. Sgt.	B
Glover S. Davis	T/4	H&S
George W. Lucas	CWO	H&S
James J. Biebighauser	Sgt.	B
Richard S. Stevick	Capt.	A
Richard J. Mason	T/3	Med.
Christian C. Lutz	Major	H&S
Joseph A. Bernier	T/4	C

Darrell C. Evans	Cpl.	A
Orlan A. Johnson	Lt. Col.	H&S

Ie Shima 16 April, 45–22 April, 45:

Charles L. Nehrbass	Pfc.	C
James W. Royston	Pfc.	B
Joseph H. Sokola	T/4	C
Norman H. Eucker	T/5	Med.
Chester C. Klinski	T/5	Med.
Arthur B. Charbonnel	Sgt.	H&S
Thomas G. Blair	1st Lt.	C
Birdell B. Dunham	T/5	B
William W. Lassetter	1st Lt.	B
Kenneth D. Holloway	S. Sgt.	C
Byron C. Hanson	1st Lt.	H&S
John Belive	T/5	H&S
Ralph Marzucca	T/4	C

BRONZE STAR (MERITORIOUS SERVICE)

All Operations

David H. Flanders	S. Sgt.	H&S
Harvey J. Field	T. Sgt.	H&S
Toivo Rajala	T/4	C
George W. Gray, Jr.	1st Lt.	A
Henry A. Lind	1st Lt.	C
Theodore C. Meinelt	Capt.	H&S
Benjamin Berschtein	Capt.	Med.
Robert K. Graham	Capt.	H&S
Henry P. Gawle	T/5	H&S
Floyd K. Oglesby	T/5	H&S
Carmen N. Muratore	S. Sgt.	H&S
Lester T. Alveshere	T/4	H&S
Bennie B. Weber	T/4	H&S
Merrill E. Blackman	M. Sgt.	H&S
Graddie Woods	M. Sgt.	H&S
Forrest H. Taylor	M. Sgt.	H&S
Clarence J. Wassenberg	T. Sgt.	H&S
Roland D. Vandale	Capt.	H&S
Robert W. Tucker	Cpl.	B
Ernest Swindlehurst	Sgt.	C
Clarence L. Carroll	T. Sgt.	H&S
Charles E. Kaylor	WOJG	H&S
Thomas J. O'Neil	Pfc.	H&S
Harold J. Proudfoot	Pfc.	H&S
Richard E. Varcoe	Pfc.	H&S
Raymond G. Brannon	S. Sgt.	H&S
Victor E. Weaver	1st Lt.	H&S

4.   COMMENDATIONS

HEADQUARTERS
292d JOINT ASSAULT SIGNAL COMPANY
APO 952, C/O POSTMASTER
San Francisco, California

22 August 1944.

SUBJECT: Commendation.

TO: Commanding Officer, 233d Engineer Combat Battalion,
               APO No. 77, c/o Postmaster, S. F. Calif.

1.   The following named enlisted men having been placed on special duty with the 292d Joint Assault Signal Company, 1 June 1944 for duty with Shore Fire Control Parties:

    T/4 Carl L. Bath
    T/4 Douglas A. Kohl
    T/4 William E. Noack
    T/4 William C. Friday
    T/4 Sheldon J. Shalett
    T/4 Gerald J. Jahnke
    T/4 John A. Bickford
    T/4 Leonard W. Pitlyk
    T/5 Stephen E. Hoffman
    T/5 William H. Orr, Jr.
    T/5 Earl J. Sanders
    T/5 Elmer H. Dessert

are commended for their work during the present operation on Guam.

2.   These men came into a strange outfit and a field that was new to them, with an attitude and effort that speaks highly for them and their organization.   They went forward after their initial landings with combat battalions and conducted themselves in their work under fire, quite creditably.   I wish to thank them and you for a job well done.

Sincerely yours,
JOHN M. McCARTY
Major, FA,
Commanding.

1st Ind.

HQ 233d ENGR COMBAT BN, APO 77, 13 Jan 45.

TO: CO, H&S Co, 233d Engr Combat Bn, APO 77.

1.   I am proud to pass on this commendation.

2.   It is this spirit of cooperation and willingness to work that enabled this battalion to do the superior job which it did throughout the operation.

ORLAN A. JOHNSON
Major, 233d Engr Combat Bn,
Commanding.

MEDICAL DETACHMENT
233d ENGINEER COMBAT BATTALION
APO 77

12 January 1945.

SUBJECT: Commendation.

TO: Commanding Officer,
         233d Engineer Combat Battalion,
         APO 77.

1. During the campaign against the enemy from 7 December 1944 to 25 December 1944, near Ipil, Leyte, P. I., the Headquarters and Service Company of your organization rendered invaluable assistance to this Detachment in the accomplishment of our missions.

2. The extreme spirit of cooperation, the unstinted use of their vehicles, the generous supply of food, kitchen facilities, cooks, and the constant volunteering of personnel as litter bearers reflects the fine spirit of cooperation of your organization, and it is the desire of the officers and men of this Detachment that our deep feelings of gratitude be expressed to the officers and men of this fine organization.

JULIUS J. SIMON,
Captain, MC,
Commanding.

HEADQUARTERS
233d ENGINEER COMBAT BATTALION
APO 77, c/o POSTMASTER
SAN FRANCISCO, CALIF.

27 January 1945

SUBJECT: Commendation.

TO: Commanding Officer, Company A, 233d Engineer Combat Battalion, APO 77.

1. It has been reported to me that Private Arnold J. Neuman of your Company completely disregarding his own personal safety by remaining at his gun, in the face of enemy strafing and bombing, on 17 December 1944 near Ipil, Leyte, P. I.

2. Personal action of this nature exemplifies the highest traditions of the service and is consistent with the high standards this Battalion has always held.

3. I desire to express my feelings of gratitude to Private Neuman, in saying, any soldier so devoted, that he places his duty before any consideration of his own personal safety, has certainly, beyond the shadow of a doubt, distinguished himself above his fellowmen.

ORLAN A. JOHNSON
Major, CE,
Commanding.

201-Neuman, Arnold J. (Enl)   1st Ind.
HEADQUARTERS COMPANY "A", 233D ENGINEER COMBAT BAT-
TALION, APO 77, c/o Postmaster, San Francisco, California, 27 January 1945.
TO: Private Arnold J. Neuman, Company A, 233d Engr Combat Bn.

It is with a great deal of pleasure that I forward this commendation. The acts herein stated are consistent with the high standards that Company "A" has always held.

RICHARD S. STEVICK
Captain,   CE
Commanding Co. "A"

A CERTIFIED TRUE COPY
VICTOR E WEAVER
1st Lt,   CE
Adjutant.

New Bern, N. C.
August 14, 1943

The Commanding General
Chesapeake Bay Sector
Fort Monroe, Va.

Dear Sir:

I wish to express my appreciation for the work that has been accomplished here on the Croatan National Forest by the engineer troops which were left behind after the maneuvers. Not only did they do an excellent job on road repair but they are also building several new bridges on the area which will be of assistance to us in fighting forest fires.

The manner in which your whole organization used National Forest lands while on maneuvers was entirely satisfactory. I would be glad to have you use the area again whenever the need arises.

Very truly yours,

C. E. KINGSLEY
District Forest Ranger
Croatan National Forest

UNITED STATES ATLANTIC FLEET
AMPHIBIOUS FORCE
AMPHIBIOUS TRAINING BASE
FORT PIERCE, FLA.

22 November 1943.

Dear Colonel Cunningham:

I have received your splendid letter of 21 November 1943 and appreciate very much the sentiments expressed in it. I wish to take this occasion to state as I have at other times that the officers and men of the 1118th Engineer Combat Group were outstanding in the performance of their duties while here and also in their conduct.

In wishing you and your officers and men the very best, I know that I am expressing not only my own feelings but the sincere good wishes of the officers and men of this base.

I hope that in the course of events in the future I shall see you and that we may be shipmates again.

Cordially and Sincerely,
C. CULBRANSON
Captain, U. S. Navy
Commanding

Colonel J. A. Cunningham, C.E., USA
Commanding 1118th Engineer Combat Group
U. S. Naval Amphibious Training Base
Fort Pierce, Florida

1st Ind.

JAC/ajb

HQ. 1118th ENGINEER COMBAT GROUP, Camp Pickett, Va., 25 November 1943.

To: Commanding Officer, 242d Engineer Combat Battalion
    "   " 132d Engineer Combat Battalion
    "   " 233d Engineer Combat Battalion
    "   " 292d Joint Assault Company

1. It is requested that basic communication and this indorsement be posted on bulletin boards.

2. I am sure that officers and men will be gratified to learn of the impression created by them during recent tour of duty at Fort Pierce, as expressed by the Commanding Officer, U. S. Navy Amphibious Training Base, in which I am proud to join.

J. A. CUNNINGHAM,
Colonel, Corps of Engineers,
Commanding.

A CERTIFIED TRUE COPY
VICTOR E WEAVER
1st Lt,   CE
Adjutant.

HEADQUARTERS 1118th ENGINEER COMBAT GROUP

Camp Pickett, Va.
20 December 1943

SUBJECT: COMMENDATION.
TO   : Commanding Officers:

> 242d Engineer Combat Battalion
> 132d Engineer Combat Battalion
> 233d Engineer Combat Battalion

1. In a recent letter to the Commanding General, 77th Infantry Division, the Commanding Officer, United States Naval Amphibious Training Base, Fort Pierce, Florida, took occasion to compliment in the highest terms the personnel of the units comprising the 1118th Engineer Combat Group. Excerpts from the letter follow:

> "During the whole training period by their hard work and keen interest in amphibious training this group proved themselves to be the most outstanding group ever sent to this Command."

> "The accomplishments of this group are due in large part to the capabilities of the officers and the soldierly qualities and discipline exhibited by the men."

2. It is requested that this letter be brought to the attention of all officers, non-commissioned officers and men, together with the thanks of the Group Commander who heartily concurs in the remarks of the Commanding Officer, United States Naval Amphibious Training Base.

J. A. CUNNINGHAM
Colonel, Corps of Engineers,
Commanding.

6 March 1944.

Lt. Col. Alexander W. Jurvic,
Headquarters 233d Engr C Bn,
Camp Pickett, Virginia.

Dear Colonel Jurvic:

Before you leave the XIII Corps, I want to express to you, and through you to your officers and men, the appreciation of this headquarters for the splendid performance of duty displayed by your organization while under this command. By careful attention to detail in training, supply, and administration, your unit has been prepared for overseas shipment and your personnel has been fitted for successful performance of your combat mission in a theater of operations.

I feel confident that although you have only recently assumed command, you will maintain in your unit the high standards of discipline and technical operations which must be required. I am confident that the record your organization attains in combat will reflect credit on the United States Army.

In all your future operations you carry with you the sincere best wishes of everyone in this headquarters.

Sincerely,
A. C. GILLEM, JR.
Major General, U. S. Army
Commanding

1st Ind

HEADQUARTERS, 233d ENGINEER COMBAT BATTALION, APO 964, c/o Postmaster, San Francisco, California

TO: Commanding Officers, Companies H&S, A, B, C, & Medics.

1.   The appreciation as expressed by General Gillem is concurred in and passed on by me.

2.   I know from personal observation that the high standards of discipline and technical operation which have been maintained in the past will be surpassed in the future.

ALEXANDER W. JURVIC,
Lt Col, 233d Engr C Bn,
Commanding.

HEADQUARTERS 77th INFANTRY DIVISION
APO No. 77, c/o Postmaster
San Francisco, California

28 June 1945

SUBJECT: Relief From Attachment to the 77th Inf. Div.

TO   :   Colonel James A. Cunningham, Corps of Engineers,

Commanding Officer 1118th Engineer Group

1.   I am writing to you in the absence of Major General A. D. BRUCE who commands this division. I know that were he present he would wish, before the division departs from its present station, to express sentiments similar to those below.

2.   It is with deep regret that I learn that your Group has been detached from the division and will not accompany us to our new station.

3.   Your Engineer Group, consisting of the 132d Engineer Combat Battalion, commanded by Major William H. HARDIN; the 233rd Engineer Combat Battalion, commanded by Lieutenant Colonel Orlan A. JOHNSON; and the 242d Engineer Combat Battalion, commanded by Lieutenant Colonel Richard G. MAROSSY, has been attached to the 77th Division ever since the fall of 1943.

4.   You and your Group of Engineer Battalions have served with the division on its amphibious training in the United States, at OAHU, and have supported it in the campaigns on GUAM, LEYTE and the RYUKYUS. In

each of these operations the officers and men of your headquarters and the battalions have given loyal, intelligent and skilful support. They have worked day and night, in sea water, mud and sand; and at GUAM they landed equipment and supplies of the division over what has been described as the most difficult reef encountered in any operation. Numerous observers who have had opportunities to see other Engineer Groups in action have stated that this division was fortunate in having with it the 1118th, which in their estimation was the best they had observed.

5.   Our association has been so long and so close that the officers and men of the division have come to think of your Group as an integral part of it, and it is with sincere regret that they learn you are not to accompany us on this next move.

6.   For its operations the 77th Division has been rather widely commended and congratulated. In simple justice we freely acknowledge the right of you and your officers and men to share with us these commendations and congratulations. No organization is any better than the officers and enlisted men who constitute it, and no high commander can be better than the troops he commands. It is my desire that every officer and every man of your splendid command, including yourself, accept the contents of this letter as applying to him as an individual as well as to the Group as such. I sincerely hope that before embarking for our next amphibious operation the 1118th Engineer Group will again be attached to the 77th Infantry Division and that together we shall succeed, as in the past, in capturing all objectives.

EDWIN H. RANDLE
Brigadier General, U. S. Army
Commanding

201.22

HEADQUARTERS 1118th ENGINEER COMBAT GROUP

APO 902, 4 July 1945

1st Ind.

To: Commanding Officer, 132d Engineer Combat Battalion
      Commanding Officer, 233d Engineer Combat Battalion
      Commanding Officer, 242d Engineer Combat Battalion
      Commanding Officer, Hq. Co. 1118th Engineer Combat Group

1. It is a distinct pleasure and a matter of great pride to forward to the officers and soldiers of the 1118th Engineer Combat Group, these words of praise by the Commanding General, 77th Infantry Division. It is gratifying to know that the hard and continuous work of all ranks is so highly appreciated.

2. It is directed that a copy of the Commanding General's letter, with this indorsement, be placed in the hands of each officer and soldier of the command.

J. A. CUNNINGHAM,
Colonel, Corps of Engineers,
Commanding.

2nd Ind

HEADQUARTERS, 233d ENGINEER COMBAT BATTALION, APO 235,

13 July 45.

TO: Officers and men of the 233d Engineer Combat Battalion.

It is truly gratifying to know that our performance of the past year is so greatly appreciated, and with the greatest of pleasure and deep pride I pass on to you, the men and officers of the 233d Engineer Combat Battalion, these words of praise, for your efforts, by the Commanding General, 77th Infantry Division.

ORLAN A. JOHNSON
Lt. Colonel   CE
Commanding.

HEADQUARTERS 1118th ENGINEER COMBAT GROUP
APO 902

4 July 1945

SUBJECT: Relief from Attachment to 77th Infantry Division.
TO   :   Brigadier General Edwin H. Randle, U. S. Army,
              Commanding, 77th Infantry Division.

1.   On behalf of all officers and soldiers of the 1118th Engineer Combat Group I am writing to thank you most warmly for your very kind letter of 28th June, upon the occasion of our relief from attachment to the Division. Our long association with the 77th had inculcated in us the feeling that we were really part of it, and made us proud. We had gloried in its achievements of the past twelve months, as we shall continue to glory in those of the future, whether or not we may be present.

2.   On its present move and forthcoming operation you and all ranks of the Division have our best wishes for a safe voyage, well earned rest and success in battle. As for ourselves, we shall continue to believe that before D-Day and H-Hour the powers-that-be will see the light and require us to take station where we rightfully belong.

3.   Again thanking you for your kindness, and assuring you of my highest personal esteem, I am

Sincerely yours,
J. A. CUNNINGHAM
Colonel, Corps of Engineers
Commanding.

1497th ENGINEER PORT CONSTRUCTION & REPAIR GROUP
APO No. 901

16 August 45

SUBJECT: Letter of Commendation.
TO: Commanding Officer, 233d Engineer Combat Battalion.

1.   On behalf of Colonel Rosenberg, Commanding Officer of the 3d Provisional Engineer Construction Brigade, and the Staff of the 1497th Engineer Port Construction and Repair Group, under whom you have served in recent months, I desire to express our profound appreciation for the cooperation and fine construction achievements during your service in the Naha Port Area. Although my own service among you has been brief, I can see on all sides the results of your efforts which have contributed much toward the successful completion of World War II.

2.   During the weeks that are immediately ahead, much remains to be done and I feel certain that the same spirit of cooperation will prompt you in your efforts to complete our task while we wait our chance to return to the good old U.S.A.

ARTHUR W. HOWSON,
Lt. Col., CE,
Commanding

5. ORGANIZATION DAY

HEADQUARTERS
233d ENGINEER COMBAT BATTALION
APO 77, c/o Postmaster
San Francisco, California

1 June 1944

GENERAL ORDERS)

                :

NUMBER   4)

1. Under the provisions of Paragraph 7, AR 345-105, the Twenty-Fifth day of January is designated as Battalion Day for the 233d Engineer Combat Battalion.

2. In as far as is practicable, all military duty will be suspended on that day. The Adjutant, 233d Engineer Combat Battalion is directed to prepare appropriate ceremonies for this occasion.

By order of Major JOHNSON:

VICTOR E. WEAVER
2d Lt, 233d Engr Combat Bn
Adjutant

OFFICIAL:
VICTOR E. WEAVER
2d Lt, 233d Engr Combat Bn
Adjutant

6. ARMY SCHOOLS

ENLISTED MEN

COMMUNICATIONS SCHOOL: Fort Monroe, Virginia
 21 February, 1943, to 10 April, 1943

Howard M. Case
Robert A. Deppe
Sumner L. Israel
John W. McGuire
Charles H. Webber

 11 April, 1943, to 9 June, 1943

Douglas A. Kohl
William C. Friday
John N. Schavilje
William E. Noack
Sheldon J. Shalett
Donald C. Allensworth
John A. Bickford

Fort DuPont, Delaware
 27 November, 1943, to 23 December, 1943

William E. Noack
Sheldon J. Shalett
John A. Bickford
Earl J. Sanders
Carl L. Bath
David Flanders
Elwood Lundberg

Camp Crowder, Missouri
 21 October, 1943, to 13 January, 1943

William H. Orr, Jr.
Elmer H. Dessert
Gerald J. Jahnke
Leonard W. Pitlyk

WATER PURIFICATION SCHOOL: Fort Belvoir, Virginia
 29 October, 1943, to 23 January, 1944

Harold Proudfoot
Chester Dubaniewicz

 20 August, 1943, to 24 November, 1943

Gordin Tobin

 14 May, 1943, to 8 August, 1943

Charlie C. Williams

SEA WATER DISTILLATION SCHOOL: Schofield Barracks, Oahu, T. H.
 28 May, 1944, to 11 June, 1944

Gordin Tobin
Fermon Waggoner
George W. DeHart

 18 June, 1944, to 28 June, 1944

Charlie C. Williams
Newell Kemp

CLASSIFICATION SCHOOL: Washington and Jefferson College, Washington, Pa.
 10 July, 1943, to 29 August, 1943

John H. Foster

ARMY ADMINISTRATION SCHOOL: University of Mississippi, Biloxi, Miss.

Milton F. Carter

SURGERY SCHOOL: Station Hospital, Fort Story, Virginia
 1 June, 1943, to 8 July, 1943

Bernice W. Vest
Richard J. Mason
Emilio C. Perretti

Camp Pickett, Virginia
 15 December, 1943, to 15 January, 1944

Medore J. Leneau

 15 January, 1944, to 13 February, 1944

Clarence E. Heller

DENTAL TECHNICIAN SCHOOL: Station Hospital, Fort Story, Virginia
 1 June, 1943, to 8 July, 1943

Ernest Jashinsky

PREVENTIVE MAINTENANCE SCHOOL: 7th Infantry Division, Schofield Barracks, Oahu
14 May, 1944, to 15 May, 1944

Lloyd K. Jones	Olaf Johanson

4 June, 1944, to 11 June, 1944

James T. Orfield	Glover S. Davis
Joseph Callahan	Walter R. Travers

11 June, 1944, to 17 June, 1944

William A. Campbell

18 June, 1944, to 24 June, 1944

Howard J. Green	Verner Erickson
Lewis J. Moore	

HEAVY EQUIPMENT SCHOOL: 7th Infantry Division, Schofield Barracks, Oahu
14 May, 1944, to 6 June, 1944

Alfred Millaway	Eugene C. Vest
Werner Hajek	Samuel Koch
Marion J. Falconburg	James R. Cardinelli

7 May, 1944, to 13 May, 1944

Raymond G. Brannon	Bennie B. Weber

11 June, 1944, to 17 June, 1944

Victor Swenders	John Morley

TRACTOR MAINTENANCE SCHOOL: 7th Infantry Division, Schofield Barracks, Oahu
18 June, 1944, to 24 June, 1944

Robert F. Brelsford	Lloyd W. Shellenbarger

AUTOMOTIVE MAINTENANCE SCHOOL: 7th Infantry Division, Schofield Barracks, Oahu
14 May, 1944, to 15 May, 1944

Otto Bogner	Guy Kincanon

ENGINEER MAINTENANCE SCHOOL: 7th Infantry Division, Schofield Barracks, Oahu
14 May, 1944, to 3 June, 1944

Graddie Woods	John T. Sells
Birdell Dunham	

ENGINEER DIESEL EQUIPMENT SCHOOL: Granite City Depot, Granite City, Illinois
4 September, 1943, to 2 December, 1943

Lloyd K. Jones	George W. Armstrong

2 August, 1943, to 2 November, 1943

Graddie Woods

AUTOMOTIVE ELECTRICIAN SCHOOL: Ord. School, Aberdeen Proving Ground, Maryland
20 September, 1943, to 2 November, 1943

Glover S. Davis

TRACTOR MECHANICS SCHOOL: Atlanta Ordnance Depot, Atlanta, Georgia
5 November, 1943, to 2 February, 1944

Lester H. Butler

5 November, 1943, to 29 February, 1944

Guy Kincanon

ENGINEER EQUIPMENT SCHOOL: Engineer School, Fort Belvoir, Virginia
28 September, 1943, to 20 November, 1943

Leonard L. Schwartz

12 November, 1943, to 12 December, 1943

Clarence Gliem	Marion J. Falconburg

GENERAL MECHANICS SCHOOL: Ordnance Automotive School, Normoyle Ord. Dep., San Antonio
3 July, 1943, to 4 November, 1943

John B. Aycock	James T. Orfield
Carl D. Snyder	Joseph E. Doiron
James H. Smith	

WELDING SCHOOL: 7th Infantry Division Welders School, Schofield Barracks, Oahu, T. H.
4 June, 1944, to 2 July, 1944

Leroy Gilkison

ORDNANCE AUTOMOTIVE SCHOOL, ATLANTA: Ordnance Depot, Atlanta, Georgia
  25 September, 1943, to 24 November, 1943
        Albert E. Donati, Jr.
  25 September, 1943, to 2 January, 1944
        Bennie B. Weber
ORDNANCE SCHOOL: Fort Crook, Nebraska
  4 September, 1943, to 3 December, 1943
        Verner Erickson
CRANE AND CATERPILLAR TRACTOR SCHOOL. Camp Bradford, Virginia
  27 December, 1943, to 5 January, 1944
        William E. Watkins   Eugene C. Vest
        Edwin Danz   Marion J. Falconburg
        Charles A. Warson   James H. Smith
MINES SCHOOL: 7th Infantry Division, Schofield Barracks, Oahu, T. H.
  30 May, 1944, to 11 June, 1944
        Harlan Middlemiss   Loren L. Kammerer
        George C. Best   Robert F. Cater
        Floyd Johnson
BOMB RECONNAISANCE AND DISPOSAL SCHOOL: Fort Shafter, Oahu, T. H.
  17 April, 1944, to 22 April, 1944
        Robert F. Cater
TRANSPORT QUARTERMASTER SCHOOL. Fort DeRussey, Waikiki, Oahu, T. H.
  14 May, 1944, to 29 May, 1944
        Merrill E. Blackman   Floyd K. Oglesby
AERIAL PHOTO INTERPRETATION: Fort Hase, Oahu, T. H.
  23 April, 1944, to 7 May, 1944
        Carl A. Senal
INSTRUCTORS' RECOGNITION SCHOOL: Fort Hase, Oahu, T. H.
  8 May, 1944, to 14 May, 1944
        Harvey J. Field
SURVEYORS' SCHOOL: Cooke Library, Punahou Campus, Oahu, T. H.
  31 May, 1944, to 1 July, 1944
        John S. T. Glenn   Joseph D. Horwitz
        Stephen Pietrzak
ENGINEER ENLISTED SPECIALISTS SCHOOL: University of Kentucky, Lexington, Kentucky
  Surveying—7 March, 1943, to 16 June, 1943
        Merrill E. Blackman
  Topographical Drafting—7 March, 1943, to 3 June, 1943
        Harvey J. Field
ENGINEER ENLISTED SPECIALISTS SCHOOL: Fort Belvoir, Virginia
  Drafting—31 July, 1943, to 4 November, 1943
        Harold Potter
ELECTRICIANS' SCHOOL: New York Trade School, New York City
  19 November, 1943, to 12 February, 1944
  Herbert Brown
7th DIVISION GENERATOR SCHOOL: Schofield Barracks, Oahu, T. H.
  4 June, 1944, to 24 June, 1944
        Herbert Arft   John F. Hunt
OFFICER CANDIDATE SCHOOL. Fort Belvoir, Virginia
        Carl A. Senal   Charles H. Kohl
        James T. Staples   George W. Schafer
COOKS AND BAKERS SCHOOL:
        Boyd Ware   Henry Weisoly
        Alfred Millaway   Edward Bennett
        William Turchick   Edward Mulligan

Frank Sutor
George Leffert
Jacob Buchwald
John Mannello
Elmer Baldwin

Thomas Petryshyn
Theodore Powell
Eugene Tambascio
Mathew Kazar
Benjamin DiBello

OFFICERS SCHOOLS

TRANSPORT QUARTERMASTER SCHOOL: Amphibious Forces, U. S. Atlantic Fleet, Camp, Bradford, Virginia—27 October, 1943, to 14 November, 1943
Byron C. Hanson

Fort DeRussey, Waikiki, Oahu, T. H.
14 May, 1944, to 29 May, 1944
Victor E. Weaver

COMMAND AND STAFF SCHOOL: Amphibious Forces, U. S. Atlantic Fleet
28 October, 1943, to 6 November, 1943
Clayton S. Gates

SECOND ARMY MINE SCHOOL: Camp Forest, Tennessee
17 November, 1943, to 2 December, 1943
Eugene E. Skogerson

7th INFANTRY DIVISION MINES SCHOOL: Schofield Barracks, Oahu, T. H.
30 May, 1944, to 11 June, 1944
George W. Gray

MORALE SERVICE SCHOOL: Punahou Campus, Honolulu, Oahu, T. H.
4 June, 1944, to 15 June, 1944
Theodore C. Meinelt

MOTOR MAINTENANCE AND HEAVY EQUIPMENT SCHOOL: Schofield Barracks, Oahu, T. H
7 May, 1944, to 3 June, 1944
Rondo W. Reusch

ENGINEER SCHOOL: Fort Belvoir, Virginia
Field Officers Course—30 August, 1943, to 9 October, 1943
Richard S Stevick

7. COMMANDERS AND STAFF

BATTALION COMMANDERS:
Lt. Col. Clayton S. Gates	1/25/43	3/4/44
Capt. Eugene E. Skogerson	3/4/44	3/6/44
Lt. Col. Alexander W. Jurvic	3/6/44	5/3/44
Lt. Col. Orlan A. Johnson	5/4/44	

EXECUTIVE OFFICERS:
Major Arthur J. Davidson	1/25/43	10/12/43
Capt. Norman B. Crumpecker	10/12/43	2/26/44
Capt. Eugene E. Skogerson	3/2/44	3/6/44
Major Orlan A. Johnson	3/6/44	5/3/44
Capt. William D. Long	5/30/44	12/4/44
Major Eugene E. Skogerson	3/7/45	

ADJUTANTS:
Lt. Theodore C. Meinelt	1/25/43	9/14/43
Lt. Thomas G. Blair	9/14/43	5/30/44
Lt. Victor E. Weaver	5/30/44	

PERSONNEL OFFICERS:
Lt. Thomas G. Blair	3/6/43	6/2/43
WOJG John F. Stemberger	5/22/43	6/16/43
WOJG Charles E. Kaylor	6/16/43	

S-2:
Lt. John E. Crain	1/25/43	7/21/43
Lt. Robert E. Caraway	7/21/43	9/1/43
Lt. Thomas G. Blair	8/19/43	9/8/43
Capt. Robert H. Sayre	9/8/43	11/19/43
Capt. Theodore C. Meinelt	11/19/43	

S-3:
Lt. Otto W. Mourek	1/25/43	3/6/43
Lt. Eric W. Myers	3/6/43	7/21/43
Lt. Christian C. Lutz	7/21/43	7/31/43
Lt. Richard S. Stevick	7/31/43	9/1/43
Lt. Thomas E. Hansen	9/1/43	9/8/43
Capt. Eugene E. Skogerson	9/8/43	3/2/44
Capt. Richard S. Stevick	3/2/44	3/6/44
Capt. Eugene E. Skogerson	3/6/44	5/22/44
Capt. William D. Long	5/22/44	5/30/44
Capt. Richard S. Stevick	5/30/44	8/27/44
Capt. Clarence E. Johnson	8/27/44	1/4/45
Major Christian C. Lutz	1/4/45	

S-4:
Lt. Thomas E. Hansen	1/25/43	9/1/43
Lt. Byron C. Hanson	9/1/43	9/8/43
Lt. Richard S. Stevick	9/8/43	10/12/43
Lt. Byron C. Hanson	10/12/43	5/30/44
Capt. Robert K. Graham	5/30/44	

ADE:
Lt. Nicholas C. Angel	6/2/43	8/12/43
Capt. Robert H. Sayre	9/5/43	9/8/43
Lt. Thomas E. Hansen	9/8/43	10/12/43
Lt. Richard S. Stevick	10/12/43	3/2/44
Lt. Otto W. Mourek	4/2/44	3/6/44
Capt. Richard S. Stevick	3/6/44	5/30/44
Lt. Otto W. Mourek	5/30/44	8/27/44
Capt. Roland D. Vandale	8/27/44	

(1) Leyte Battalion Officers, February, 1945. Colonel Cunningham, CO, 1118th Group, in the center. (2) Battalion Officers, (3) The Battalion Staff. (4) Commanding Officers.

(1) S-1 Section; Personnel Section; (2) S-2, S-3, ADE Sections. (3) S-4 Section.
(4) The Pillrollers.

ASST. S-2:

Lt. Robert E. Caraway	6/2/43	7/10/43
Lt. Thomas G. Blair	7/10/43	8/19/43
Lt. Thomas G. Blair	9/8/43	9/14/43
Lt. Theodore C. Meinelt	9/14/43	11/19/43
Lt. Peter J. Langhans	3/2/44	4/3/44
Lt. Frederick W. Bloomfield	4/3/44	11/29/44
Lt. Gerald L. Kock	3/17/45	6/13/45
Lt. John Hude	1/4/45	

ASST. S-3:

Lt. Romaine S. Foss	3/6/43	6/2/43
Lt. William W. Lassetter	6/2/43	7/31/43
Lt. Otto W. Mourek	10/2/43	3/2/44
Lt. Martin V. Szivulka	3/2/44	3/6/44
Lt. Otto W. Mourek	3/6/44	4/14/44
Lt. Carl C. Cook	4/14/44	8/27/44
Lt. Romaine S. Foss	8/27/44	1/4/45
Lt. Otto W. Mourek	1/4/45	

ASST. S-4:

Lt. Raymond W. Naseman	3/20/43	5/25/43
Lt. Byron C. Hanson	9/8/43	10/12/43
CWO George Lucas	3/6/43	

RECON.:

Lt. Thomas G. Blair	6/2/43	7/10/43
Lt. Robert E. Caraway	7/10/43	7/21/43
Lt. Eric W. Myers	10/2/43	1/15/44
Lt. Victor E. Weaver	3/2/44	5/30/44
Lt. Allen K. Reid	5/30/44	4/4/45

MOTOR OFFICERS:
Lt. Rondo W. Ruesch	1/25/43	10/18/43
WOJG Seton E. Hackworth	10/22/43	1/29/44
Lt. Rondo W. Ruesch	1/29/44	6/13/45
Lt. George W. Gray	6/13/45	

ASST. MOTOR OFFICER:
WOJG Seton E. Hackworth	1/29/44	2/17/45

DENTAL OFFICER:
Capt. Myron I. Price	5/12/43	5/22/44
Capt. Benjamin Birschtein	5/22/44	

BATTALION SURGEONS:
Capt. Julius J. Simon	1/25/43	8/17/45
Capt. Benjamin F. Levy	8/17/45	

COMPANY A

COMMANDING OFFICERS:
Lt. James S. Beyer	1/25/43	3/6/43
Lt. Eugene E Skogerson	3/6/43	9/8/43
Lt. John E. Crain	9/8/43	10/16/43
Capt. Clarence E. Johnson	10/16/43	8/27/44
Capt. Richard S. Stevick	8/27/44	6/29/45
Lt. Harley T. Crawford	6/29/45	

PLATOON LEADERS:
Lt. Christian C. Lutz	1/25/43	7/21/43
Lt. John W. Petre, Jr.	1/25/43	3/6/43
Lt. Roland D. Vandale	1/25/43	7/31/43
Lt. Mike Cassis	3/6/43	10/18/43
Lt. Byron C. Hanson	3/6/43	9/1/43
Lt. Henry A. Lind	3/6/43	7/31/43
Lt. Eric W. Myers	7/21/43	10/2/43
Lt. Otto W. Mourek	7/21/43	9/14/43
Lt. Clarence E. Johnson	7/21/43	10/16/43
Lt. William D. Mitchell	7/31/43	1/15/44
Lt. Max L. Daley	9/14/43	3/2/45
Lt. John W. Martell	10/2/43	1/15/44
Lt. Raymond W. Naseman	10/12/43	1/15/44
Lt. Rondo W. Ruesch	10/18/43	1/29/44
Lt. George W. Gray	1/29/44	6/13/45
Lt. Carl C. Cook	1/29/44	4/14/44
Lt. John Hude	2/10/44	3/18/44
Lt. Romaine S. Foss	3/18/44	8/27/44
Lt. Otto W. Mourek	4/14/44	5/30/44
Lt. Charles E. Schaub	7/2/44	4/10/45
Lt. Carl C. Cook	8/27/44	12/27/44
Lt. Peter J. Langhans	1/4/45	4/10/45
Lt. Allen K. Reid	4/4/45	
Lt. Frank A. Vajda	6/13/45	
Lt. Gerald L. Koch	6/13/45	

COMPANY B

COMMANDING OFFICERS:
Lt. Nicholas C. Angel	1/25/43	6/2/43
Lt. Robert H. Sayre	3/6/43	9/5/43
Capt. Norman G. Crumpecker	9/5/43	10/12/43
Capt. Roland D. Vandale	10/12/43	8/27/44
Lt. Otto W. Mourek	8/27/44	1/4/45
Capt. Clarence E. Johnson	1/4/45	

PLATOON LEADERS:

Lt. Murrey W. Fuller	1/25/43	6/2/43
Lt. Clarence E. Johnson	1/25/43	3/5/43
Lt. Richard S. Stevick	1/25/43	6/2/43
Lt. Otto W. Mourek	3/6/43	7/31/43
Lt. James S. Beyer	3/6/43	3/10/43
Lt. Raymond W. Naseman	3/6/43	3/20/43
Lt. William D. Mitchell	3/6/43	7/31/43
Lt. Raymond W. Naseman	5/25/43	10/16/43
Lt. Romaine S. Foss	6/2/43	3/18/44
Lt. Roland D. Vandale	7/31/43	10/12/43
Lt. William W. Lassetter	7/31/43	9/24/45
Lt. Henry A. Lind	7/31/43	10/2/43
Lt. Robert K. Graham	9/20/43	5/30/44
Lt. John Hude	10/12/43	2/10/44
Lt. Frederick W. Bloomfield	1/29/44	4/3/44
Lt. John Hude	3/18/44	1/4/45
Lt. Peter J. Langhans	4/3/44	1/4/45
Lt. Byron C. Hanson	5/30/44	6/29/45
Lt. Romaine S. Foss	1/4/45	
Lt. Clarence J. Wangerin	6/14/45	

COMPANY C

COMMANDING OFFICERS:

Lt. Eugene E. Skogerson	1/25/43	3/6/43
Lt. Robert K. Graham	3/6/43	9/20/43
Capt. Christian C. Lutz	9/20/43	1/4/45
Capt. John W. Petre, Jr.	1/4/45	

PLATOON LEADERS:

Lt. Eric W. Myers, Jr.	1/25/43	3/6/43
Lt. Mike Cassis	1/25/43	3/6/43
Lt. Robert E. Caraway	2/3/43	3/6/43
Lt. Clarence E. Johnson	3/6/43	7/31/43
Lt. John W. Petre, Jr.	3/6/43	1/4/45
Lt. Harley T. Crawford	3/6/43	6/22/45
Lt. John W. Martell	3/6/43	10/2/43
Lt. William W. Lassetter	3/6/43	6/2/43
Lt. Murray W. Fuller	6/2/43	1/15/44
Lt. Christian C. Lutz	7/31/43	9/20/43
Lt. Henry A. Lind	10/20/43	
Lt. Allen K. Reid	1/29/44	5/30/44
Lt. Thomas G. Blair	5/30/44	
Lt. Rondo W. Ruesch	6/13/45	
Lt. Robert E. Jackson	8/25/45	

HEADQUARTERS AND SERVICE COMPANY

COMMANDING OFFICERS:

Lt. Norman G. Crumpecker	1/25/43	9/5/43
Capt. Nicholas C. Angel	9/5/43	6/22/45
Lt. Harley T. Crawford	6/22/45	6/29/45
Lt. Byron C. Hanson	6/29/45	9/24/45
Lt. William W. Lassetter	9/24/45	

OFFICERS:

Lt. Robert E. Caraway	3/6/43	6/2/43
Lt. Max L. Daley	3/6/43	9/14/43
Lt. Nicholas C. Angel	4/19/43	6/2/43
CWO George Lucas	5/16/43	
Lt. Richard S. Stevick	6/2/43	7/31/43

Lt. Nicholas C. Angel	8/12/43	9/5/43
Lt. Richard S. Stevick	8/1/43	9/8/43
Lt. Otto W. Mourek	9/14/43	10/2/43
Lt. Mike Cassis	9/14/43	10/30/43
Lt. George W. Gray	1/7/44	1/29/44
Lt. Emmett Donohue	1/7/44	1/15/44
Lt. Frederick W. Bloomfield	1/18/44	1/29/44
Lt. Allen K. Reid	1/18/44	1/29/44
Lt. Carl C. Cook	1/28/44	1/29/44
Lt. Peter J. Langhans	2/25/44	3/2/44
Lt. Victor E. Weaver	2/25/44	3/2/44
Lt. Martin V. Szivulka	2/25/44	3/2/44

8. HIGHER HEADQUARTERS

Assigned to E.D.C., First Army	3 Jan. 43
Attached to C.B.S.	11 Jan. 43
Attached to M.F., C.B.S. (111th RCT)	25 Jan. 43
Relieved from E.D.C., First Army	13 Sept. 43
Assigned to XIII Corps, A.G.F.	13 Sept. 43
Attached to 77th Inf. Div. and 1118th Engr. Combat Gp.	13 Sept. 43
Relieved from XIII Corps, A.G.F.	12 Mar. 44
Assigned to IX Service Command	12 Mar. 44
Assigned to CPA	21 Mar. 44
Assigned to XXIV Corps	21 Mar. 44
Assigned to CPBC	
Assigned to SPBC	1 Nov. 44
Assigned to Sixth Army	
Assigned to Eighth Army	26 Dec. 44
Attached to XXIV Corps	2 Feb. 45
Assigned to Tenth Army	10 Feb. 45
Assigned to ISCOM 331 for Operational Control	21 Apr. 45
Attached to 1st Engr. Special Brigade for Operational Control	20 Apr. 45
Attached to 1st Engr. Special Brigade	1 May 45
Attached for Operations to XXIV Corps, S.P.	1 May 45
1st Platoon of Company "C" attached to Kerama Retto	24 May 45
Attached to 77th Inf. Div.	19 Jun. 45
Attached to ISCOM 331	22 Jun. 45
Attached to 1497th Engr. Port Construction and Repair Gp.	21 Jun. 45
Assigned A.G.F., APO 331	29 Jun. 45
Assigned to 3d POA Prov. Engr. Construction Brigade	30 Jul. 45
Attached to 1181 Engr. Construction Gp.	5 Aug. 45
Assigned to 427th Engr. Construction Gp.	13 Aug. 45
Assigned to 1497th Engr. Port Construction and Repair Gp.	20 Aug. 45
Assigned to Sixth Army	15 Aug. 45

9. SUBORDINATE ATTACHED UNITS

7th Beach Battalion, U.S.N.

Attached per par. 2, Special Order No. 108, dated 16 October, 1943, headquarters 233d Engineer Combat Bn. Relieved per par. 4 Special Order No. 119, dated 27 November, 1943, Headquarters 233d Engineer Combat Bn. effective 20 November, 1943. *Training at Fort Pierce N.A.T.B., Florida.*

292d Joint Assault Signal Company, Shore Beach Communication Sections:

June 25, 1944, to August 1, 1944................................Guam Operation
December 5, 1944, to January 1, 1945.........................Ormoc Bay Landing

10. LIST OF SHIPS

Seattle to Hawaii.....................USAT *Noordam*........................Bn.
Hawaii to Guam......................USS *Monrovia*........................Bn. Hq.
                                 USS *Alcione*..........................Co. A
                                 USS *Funston*.........................Co. B
                                 USS *War Hawk*......................Co. C
                                 USS *China Victory*...................TQM Team
Guam to Leyte.......................USS *Elmore*.........................Bn. Hq.
                                 USS *Harris*...........................Co. A
                                 USS *Herald of Morning*............Co. B
                                 USS *Barnstable*......................Co. C
Leyte to Okinawa....................USS *Goodhue*.......................Bn. Hq.
                                 USS *Montrail*........................Co. A
                                 USS *Eastland*........................Co. B
                                 USS *Telfair*..........................Co. C
                                 USS *Wyandot*.......................TQM Team
Okinawa to Japan....................*LST 687*..............................Bn.

11. ROSTERS

233d ENGINEER COMBAT BATTALION

OFFICERS

Nicholas C. Angel
James S. Beyer
Benjamin Birchstein
Thomas G. Blair
Frederick W. Bloomfield
Robert E. Caraway
Mike Cassis
Carl C. Cook
John E. Crain
Harley T. Crawford
Lawrence E. Creasy
Norman G. Crumpecker
Max L. Daley
Arthur J. Davidson
Michael B. Dubey

Romaine S. Foss
Murrey W. Fuller
Clayton S. Cates
Robert K. Graham
George W. Gray
Seton E. Hackworth
Thomas E. Hansen
Byron C. Hanson
John Hude
Robert E. Jackson
Clarence A. Johnson
Orlan A. Johnson
Alexander W. Jurvic
Charles E. Kaylor
Gerald L. Koch

Peter J. Langhans
William W. Lassetter
Benjamin F. Levy, Jr.
Henry A. Lind
William D. Long
George Lucas
Christian C. Lutz
Jack O. Lynch
John W. Martell
Theodore C. Meinelt
William D. Mitchell
Otto W. Mourek
Eric W. Myers, Jr.
Eugene P. Myers
Raymond W. Noseman

Roger D. Olleman
John W. Petre, Jr.
Myron I. Price
Allen K. Reid
Rondo W. Ruesch
Robert H. Sayre
Charles E. Schaub
Julius J. Simon
Eugene E. Skogerson
Raymond J. Staffa
Richard S. Stevich
Frank A. Vajda
Roland D. Vandale
Edward C. Vaughn
Clarence J. Wangerin
Victor E. Weaver

ENLISTED MEN

HEADQUARTERS & SERVICE COMPANY

Andrew F. Acker
Mathias M. Adler
Leonard Alexonis
Donald Allensworth
Samuel A. Alloy
Lester T. Alveshere
George R. Armstrong
Harold M. Arnenson
Charles Augelli
Alfred R. Baer
Mark P. Baeten
Enrico V. Ballezzi
Charles E. Barnett
John A. Batdorf
Carl L. Bath
Shirley D. Batron
Henry E. Baumdraber
Linus G. Becker
Walter W. Belden
John Belive
Edward J. Bennett
Herman A. Bergen
Daniel M. Besaw

George W. Betchel
John A. Bickford
Kennard V. Bigelow
Kenneth V. Bigelow
Merrill Blackman
Hugh P. Blanford
Raymond J. Bohen
William A. Bowron
Louis S. Bozin
John F. Brandenburg
Raymond G. Brannon
Mervin L. Branson
Keith E. Brayton
Thomas P. Brendle
Herbert E. Brown
William L. Broyles
Calvin J. Buehrer
Floyd L. Bullard
James J. Burke
Omar L. Burkgren
Earl J. Burrell
Oliver H. Bushman
Alfonso Carlini

Alvin A. Card
Andrew Carlon
Peter J. Carocci
Clarence L. Carroll
Milton J. Carter
Robert F. Cater
Paul E. Champagne
Arthur Charbonnel
Ferris B. Choate
Donald K. Christenson
Frederick K. Classen
Carl T. Colaianni
James R. Conley
Thomas A. Conlon
Kenneth M. Cook
Robert H. Cook
Ygnacio Cortez
Cloyce V. Culver
Steve A. Cvaniga
Glover S. Davis
James A. Davis
John L. Davis
Peter A. DeBlonk

George W. DeHart
Joe A. DeHerrera
Joseph DeMaida
Robert A. Deppe
Elmer H. Dessert
Harlan L. Dicks
Fred J. Dillbert
Russell W. Dimon
James W. Dixon
Harold F. Doan
Bruno Dombroski
Earl F. Donahue
Joseph B. Doiron
Albert E. Donati, Jr.
Patrick H. Donohue
Harry Drabkin
Raymond J. Droste
Chester M. Dubaniewicz
Richard W. DuBois
Virgil Duff, Sr.
Birdell B. Dunham
Calvin L. Dunlevy
Ira E. Durham
John T. Dyer

(1) Headquarters and Service Company. (2) Headquarters Platoon. (3) Motor Pool. (4) Medical Detachment

Elmore B. Edwards	Glade L. Hanes	Edward J. Kennedy	Dean R. Mack
Homer E. Eickholdt	Cecil L. Hastings	Walter L. Kennon	Raymond T. Majewski
Arthur W. Eppinger	Francis J. Heinrich	Norman A. King	Robert R. Mannis
Verner G. Erickson	Allen C. Hektner	Robert H. King	Lino Marchetti
James A. Evans	Clarence E. Heller	Robert H. Klein	Herman R. Martin
Bertrand L. Feldmier	Montgomery Henderson	Chester C. Klinski	Richard J. Mason
Harvey J. Field	Walter S. Hendzel	Richard C. Knowlton	Herbert W. McCarty
William K. Fite	Gustave L. Henriksen	Douglas A. Kohl	Thomas McCreadie
Gerald J. Fitzgerald	Bernard R. Hill	Richard J. Kopic	Arthur R. McEllen
David H. Flanders	Arthur M. Holm	John C. Kos	James W. McGinnis
John J. Foster	David Hom	Jack E. Koster	Raymond J. McGowan
Robert W. Francois	George E. Hopkins, Jr.	Sylvester P. Kozlowski	John W. McGuire
William C. Friday	John K. House	Herbert E. Krier	Donald R. McLeod
Clarence C. Furlough	Elmer J. Urban	Joseph Kritz	Robert W. Mead
Joseph Gallo	Joseph D. Horowitz	Alfred W. Kruck, Jr.	Kenneth E. Means
Norbert J. Ganter	James Hubeny	Clement F. Kryspin	Ervin H. Meeker
Henry P. Gawle	Dean E. Hunter	Bernard B. Lacina	Robert B. Meeker
John L. Gerst	William B. Ide, Jr.	Albert L. Lafferty	Delmar D. Meints
Nelson Gesser	Sumner L. Israel	Melvin E. Laizure	Howard W. Mesecher
Albert E. Giacin	Ernest Jashinsky	Anthony A. Lamacki	William A. Meurer
John A. Gilbertsen	Fred B. Jacobson	Edward G. Lankowski	Thaddeus S. Micek
Vernon Gibbard	Jack D. Johnson	Robert E. Laprise	Edmond T. Mieszczur
Leecoy S. Gilkison	Kermit W. Johnson	Warren E. Lauer	John M. Miholic
William A. Goad	Sidney P. Johnson, Jr.	Raymond T. Laurion	Robert K. Mika
Peter J. Gogen	Wallace M. Johnson	Arthur W. Lechner, Jr.	Wendell Miller
Joseph S. Goldsmith	Clifford A. Jones	Carl W. Ledin	Warren C. Mitchell
Augustine L. Gomez	Herbert H. Jones	George E. Ledo	Joseph B. Mocke
Robert Goulet	Lloyd K. Jones	Clarence J. Leiber	Irving E. Mochrke
Clarence E. Gower	Harold A. Juergens	Orville F. Leidt	William J. Moede
Lynford N. Grandon	Frank D. Jurenic	Medore J. Leneau	Correl W. Mommaerts
Robert N. Grefe	Leo C. Kalious	Milton Levey	William F. Moore
Stephen Grgas	Robert H. Kammerer	Dwaine R. Lewis	John Morley
Danny J. Griffen	Anton L. Kasprowicz	Elwood H. Lundberg	Harold J. Mudloff
Isaac E. Guinn	Wayne M. Keebaugh	Edmund J. Lumas	Carmen N. Muratore
Tom M. Hadfield	George M. Kelley	William J. MacArthur	Clarence E. Nedrow
Dennis Handley	Newell L. Kemp	Robert W. MacGregor	Arnold J. Neuman

Edwin W. Neveu
Paul J. Niemi
William E. Noack
Warren J. Norrgard
Zigmond J. Novak
Floyd K. Oglesby
Daniel F. O'Leary
Glenn E. Olson
William H. Orr, Jr.
Adolph M. O'Seka
Donald W. Osenga
Amel E. Ott
Bernard H. Oudeans
Joseph Parijczuk
Michael S. Pavolic
Emilio C. Perretti
Kenneth G. Perry
Francis G. Peters
Arthur L. Peterson
Garfield R. Peterson
Homer C. Peterson
Joseph W. Petrovic
Wallace H. Peterson
Robert N. Pflonzer
Orleen V. Piccirilli
Richard T. Pierce
Walter M. Pietraszek
Stephen P. Pietrzak
Joseph Pinsonneault
Leonard W. Pitlyk
Gwindlyn H. Platt
Carl E. Pleger
Ellsworth D. Pool
Frank Popper, Jr.
Harold N. Potter
Theodore A. Powell
John V. Powers
Donald E. Price
Albert R. Primrose
William L. Proctor
Harold J. Proudfoot
George E. Rafferty
William E. Raines

Gilbert R. Randall
Chasten J. Randolph
Charles S. Ratzloff
Edward A. Rekar
Richard H. Rengstorf, Jr.
William A. Rice
Albert Richards
Raymond Richardson
Emil F. Rizzi
Dwight E. Robe
John M. Rodriques
Ronald J. Rooney
Leonard J. Root
Michael L. Roscia
Adolph J. Rosol
James W. Roysten
Raymond J. Rudd
James H. Rusk
Gerald M. Ryan
Robert J. Ryan
William J. Rymer
Leonard F. Sager
Carroll P. Saley
Earl J. Sanders
George W. Schaefer
John N. Schavilje
Allan R. Scheer
Robert L. Scheibl
Gaile H. Schirmer
Charles J. Schley
Walter H. Schmidt
Clarence R. Schmit
Victor Scotto
Robert G. Scrutchfield
John T. Sells
Carl A. Senal
Edward J. Senkeleski
Claude O. Senser
Edward C. Seybold
Sheldon J. Shalett
Joseph P. Shovlin
Samuel E. Siegel
Edward H. Sidell

Sarkis C. Simitian
Joseph L. Simmet
Clark R. Simon
Abner H. Smith
Leroy Smith
Richard H. Smith
Robert E. Smith
John A. Snodgrass
David L. Snow
Eugene J. Sollie
Orville J. Sorensen
Robert K. Sorensen
Richard Southworth
Charles H. Spices
Gene E. Stafford
James T. Staples
Allen W. Starr
Albert R. Stauss
Alex A. Steiner
Paul Stengel
Duane R. Stevenson
Robert C. Strejc
Donald W. Sullivan
Harland A. Swager
Marvin R. Sykes
Everett L. Tabor
Joseph J. Tarasewicz
Forrest H. Taylor, Jr.
Lawrence E. Tennity
Ted B. Theodorsen
Donald A. Thompson
Raymond J. Thompson
George W. Thornton
Don A. Tippen
Gordon R. Tobin
Moses A. Totty
Walter R. Travers
Robert W. Tucker
William Turchick
Troy M. Turman
Norman H. Uecker
Fred B. Underwood
John J. Urbanski

Bonnie D. Valdez
John J. VanHorn
Richard E. Varcoe
Charles W. Vaughn
Joseph A. Vermette
Bernice W. Vest
Eugene C. Vest
Louis J. Vitale
James P. Vizzard
Fermon Waggoner
Francis F. Walker
Bernard J. Walsh
Robert C. Wasback
Maurice D. Wasmuth
Clarence J. Wassenberg
Arthur J. Watson
Charles J. Webber
Bonnie B. Weber
Lyle H. Wendorf
Fenon M. Weyna
Albert F. Wheeldon
Francis E. White
Joe R. Whiteside
John J. Wielgus
Charlie C. Williams
Alan M. Wilson
Hamilton Wilson
Harold E. Wiltse
Wilbert L. Wirolo
Edwin A. Witowski
Edward G. Wokas
Gordon N. Wood
Graddie Woods
Lawrence J. Yarmoska
Harold Yoblong
Isreal J. Yogman
Myron C. Youmans
Charles E. Young
Raymond P. Zaworotney
Stanley J. Zelmanski
Arthur J. Zeigler
Theodore Zhyowoski

MEDICAL DETACHMENT

Shirley D. Batron
Earl J. Burrell
Clarence E. Daves
Robert G. Delaney
Robert W. Francois
Norbert J. Ganter
John S. Glenn

Dennis Handley
Clarence E. Heller
David Hom
Ernest Jashinsky
Wallace M. Johnson
Clifford A. Jones
Chester C. Klinski

Charles F. Kohl
Robert E. La Prise
Medore J. Leneau
James W. McGinnis
Richard J. Mason
John M. Miholi
William J. Moede

Emilio C. Perretti
Michael L. Roschia
Samuel E. Siegel
Robert C. Strejc
Don A. Tippen
Norman H. Uecker
Bernice W. Vest

(1) Company A. (2) Headquarters Platoon. (3) 1st Platoon. (4) 2d Platooon.
(5) 3d Platoon.

COMPANY "A"

Walter Abood
John Q. Adams
Clark E. Adney
Leonard M. Alexonis
Donald C. Allensworth
Charles D. Amero
Albert E. Anderson
Herbert C. Arft
George R. Armstrong
Paul S. Arno
John B. Aycock
Salvatore Badalamente
Daryl E. Baker
Douglas G. Baker
John G. Bakirdgis
Fred J. Barron
Carl L. Bath
William H. Bayless, II
Jack O. Beason
Howard J. Benicker
Chester A. Bennett
Joseph A. Berge
Charles F. Bergmann
Sylvio P. Bianchi
Harold Bishop
Merill E. Blackman
Robert J. Blondin
Vincent J. Bolt
Livio M. Bonaldi
William A. Bowron
George H. Braver
Axel O. Broander
Eugene F. Brock
Thomas J. Brophy
Arthur E. Bryans

Frank A. Buda
Edwin A. Budnick
Omar L. Burkgren
Phillip E. Burnett
William Bush
Oliver H. Bushman
Roy T. Calloway
Alvin A. Card
Verda L. Carney
Peter J. Carocci
Clarence L. Carroll
John F. Carroll
Charles J. Catalano
James F. Cervant
Warren W. Chamberlain
Donald K. Christenson
Frank E. Ciesielski
Charles A. Clark
Anthony L. Cocuzzo
William H. Collier
Thomas A. Conlin
Robert H. Cook
Ben Cooper
Ygnacio Cortez
Clinton P. Cummings
Josiah H. Curtis
Frank L. Cutrone
George F. Cvitanov
Sigmund A. Czekalski
William R. Dalton
Charles E. Damoth
Harvey P. Darling
Glover S. Davis
George W. DeHart
Robert G. Delaney

Joseph DeMaida
Robert A. Deppe
Lawrence W. Derrick
Donald L. Dixon
Daniel J. Donnelly
John V. Donnelly
Harry Drabkin
Raymond J. Droste
Richard W. DuBois
Calvin L. Dunlevy
Donald W. Elliott
Johnny D. Enfield
Rocco Ensero
Gerald F. Ensman
Verner G. Erickson
Darrell C. Evans
Ernest N. Evans
Leroy A. Fauset, IV
Joseph Fink
Anthony Franciosi, Jr.
Wayne G. Francisco
Cary M. Friend
Harold G. Frost
Kenneth W. Fruehauf
Joseph Gallo
Melvin J. Gardner
John J. Getz
Albert E. Giacin
Vernon Gibbard
Irwin L. Gibbs
John S. Glenn
Clarence H. Gliem
Augustine L. Gonrey
Jose G. Gonzales
James P. Goodwin

Glen A. Govin
Lynford N. Grandon
Robert L. Greene
Gerald A. Greengtski
Stephen W. Grgas
Glenwood W. Griewahn
Danny J. Griffen
Harry A. Grzenkowicz
Frank A. Guidice
Werner J. Hajek
John Halrunk
George B. Hamling
Herman A. Hanson
Martin F. Hanson
Ivy L. Harmon
Albert J. Hart
Peter T. Heckler
Francis J. Heinrich
Allen C. Hektner
Charles C. Herb
David C. Holmes
David Hom
Kenneth H. Hovdeness
James Hubeny
Chauncey W. Ingersoll
Joseph F. Izworski
Gerald J. Jahnke
Charles J. Jelinek
William Jenezon, Jr.
Jay L. Jenne
Olaf H. Johanson
Lloyd K. Jones
Robert E. Jones
Frank D. Jurenic
Theodore W. Kalen

Earl G. Kelm
Edward J. Kennedy
Walter L. Kennon
Roy A. Killam
Floyd C. Kimmel
Robert H. King
George Klatt
Robert H. Klein
Chester C. Klinski
William Knapp
Dwight V. Knauss
Cletus R. Konst
Richard J. Kopic
John C. Kos
George A. Kramer
Raymond G. Kuhlman
Harold W. Kutz
Anthony A. Lamacki
Rollen G. Lambert
Ralph C. La Porte
Ervin E. Lasley
Warren E. Lauer
Carl W. Ledin, Jr.
John L. Lentz
Mervin F. Leonard
Jack M. Lewis
Leland L. Lewis
Ezra J. Loftin
Elwood H. Lundberg
William J. MacArthur
Bernard J. McCafferty
Thomas V. McCarthy
Bert McCrandall
George E. McDannold
Raymond J. McGowan
William J. Machir
Frank B. MacIntosh
Leslie D. McVay
Raymond T. Majewski
John G. Mannello
Robert R. Mannis
Lino Marchetti
Frank C. Marini
Charles E. Marquis
Richard J. Mason
Joe J. Masten

Frank M. Matzke
Frank Medved
Charles A. Meecham
Domenic Melillo
Warren P. Melliger
Carl E. Merritt
Erwin H. Mettler
Edward F. Micek
Harlan W. Middlemiss
John M. Miholic
Alfred W. Millaway, Jr.
James C. Miller
Raymond W. Miller
John P. Mlynarczyk
Irving E. Moehrke
Matthew M. Monczynski
Herman Monroe
Lewis J. Moore
Thomas J. Morrison
Harold J. Mudloff
Dean D. Mueller
Walter J. Murphy
Clarence E. Nedrow
Claude J. Neil
Robert C. Nelson
Arnold J. Neuman
Edwin W. Neven
Raymond M. Newquist
Waldo R. Nickel
William E. Noack
Warren J. Norrgard
Robert W. O'Donnell
Harold C. Oliver
Earl A. Oltersdorf
William H. Orr, Jr.
Adolph M. O'Seka
Joseph G. Ott
Francis H. Paddock
Eldon E. Palmer
Joseph Parijczuk
John G. Pasquale
Michael S. Pavolic
Francis G. Peters
Garfield R. Peterson
Homer C. Peterson
Robert W. Peterson

Joseph W. Petrovic
Clarence E. Petz
Robert N. Pflanger
Dorsie J. Phipps
Walter M. Pietraszek
Joseph A. Pinsonneault
Sam Pizzuto
Harold N. Potter
William L. Proctor
Hughie P. Quinn
George E. Rafferty
Gilbert R. Randall
Francis X. Rankin
David C. Rapp
LeRoy G. Reason
Richard H. Rengstorff
Albert Riniker
Vito Rizzi
Erskine F. Roberts
Ronald J. Rooney
Victor A. Roskey
Raymond J. Rudd
William J. Rymer
Frederico Sandoval
Allen R. Scheer
Robert L. Scheibl
Howard G. Scheidle
Johnie A. Schepers
William A. Schloff
Richard Schmidt
William J. Schoph
Clarence R. Schmit
Roy R. Schoenherr
Roy A. Schroeder
John A. Schultz
Frank J. Seiroki
Edward C. Seybold
Harold N. Shaffer
Sheldon J. Shalett
Rupert R. Sheumaker
Joseph P. Shovlin
David B. Silverberg
Vernon Sir-Basil Ice
Ralph E. Sisco
Frank C. Skellen
Robert L. Smith

Carl D. Snyder, Jr.
Jack Soldani
William J. Sopko
Richard N. Southworth
Ralph S. Sprague
Linwood H. Stanfield
James T. Staples
Alex A. Steiner
Raymond E. Stieben
Clifford V. Stienvalt
Harry Strauch
Walter R. Sutliff
Jarrell D. Sweeney
John M. Tanner
Guy D. Taylor
Ralph D. Thomas
George W. Thornton
Orville F. Tiedt
Don A. Tippen
Moses A. Totty
Noland L. Twiddy
Elmer J. Urban
Ramon R. Valadez
Mike Vialpando
Ricardo J. L. Vigil
Victor A. Walker
Boyd L. Ware
Arthur J. Watson
Edgar N. Watters
Ervin F. Wenger
Ralph N. West
Frank L. Wever
Emil H. Wildaver
Floyd E. Wilkins
Edward J. Williams
Robert A. Wilson
Norman G. Wirick
Edwin W. Witowski
Charles R. Wolverton
Bonnie E. Wyatt
Myron C. Youmans
Charles E. Young
Henry Yunek
Alphonse Zakolski
Louis J. Zanon
Raymond P. Zaworonty

COMPANY "B"

Andrew F. Acker
Roger S. Adams
Mathias M. Adler
William Albershardt
Charles Ambrosio
Leland L. Anderson
Harold Arenson
George R. Armstrong
George W. Armstrong
Kenneth R. Armstrong
Paul S. Arno
Michael Autera

Lynn Albertson
Frank Babiarz
Alfred R. Baer
Mark P. Baeten
Elmer M. Baldock
Clarence R. Ballantine
Elmer G. Baldwin
Jose E. Barela
Arthur A. Barnes
Jerome J. Barnett
Harold A. Becker
Fred Beckmeyer

Howard I. Benicker
Daniel M. Besaw
George C. Best
John A. Bickford
James J. Biebighauser
Vincint J. Bielecki
Kennard V. Bigelow
Albert P. Bollig
Daniel V. Bostrom
Arthur R. Bovino
John F. Brandenburg
Raymond G. Brannon

Mervin L. Branson
William Brassfield
Kieth E. Brayton
Robert F. Brelsford
Roy R. Brenizer
Oliver H. Buchman
Otho J. Buckley
Calvin J. Buehrer
James W. Bunten
Dellos B. Burgett
Lester H. Butler
George A. Campbell

(1) Company B.   (2) Headquarters Platoon.   (3) 1st Platoon.   (4) 2d Platoon.
(5) 3d Platoon.

Alfonso Carlini	Patrick H. Donohue	Lynford N. Grandon	Henry A. Janicki
Melvin W. Carnes	Robert T. Donaldson	Howard J. Green	Ernest Jashinsky
Paul Caulkins	John J. Downes	Robert N. Grefe	Francis C. Johnson
Arthur Charbonnel	Harold J. Driscoll	Stephen W. Grgas	Gustof A. Johnson
Ferris B. Choate	Virgil Duff, Sr.	Danny J. Griffen	Harry A. Johnson, Jr.
Edward Christensen	Birdell B. Dunham	Lawrence E. Guard	Kermit W. Johnson
Marshall Christian, Jr.	Leon A. Dunsmore	Isaac E. Guinn	Sidney P. Johnson, Jr.
Jack E. Clark	Ira E. Durham	Robert L. Guthrie	Leo C. Kalious
Frederick K. Classen	Weldon H. Edwards	William Haragan	Loren L. Kammerer
Raymond Clemmons	Frank S. Elm	Albert J. Hart	Erick A. Kangas
James R. Conley	Arthur W. Eppinger	Cecil L. Hastings	Hubert E. Kangas
Bert L. Coon	Victor H. Fail	Rex Hawk	Wayne M. Keebaugh
Hubert A. Copeland	Marion J. Falconburg	Peter T. Heckler	Roland P. Kelley
Ygnacio Cortez	Bernard Q. Banell	Melvin L. Hedlund	Thomas J. Kessler
George J. Costa	William A. Ferris	Allen C. Hektner	Floyd C. Kimmel
John T. Cox	Lester H. Ficke	James R. Hendricks	Robert H. King
Kenneth W. Cramton	Harvey J. Field, Jr.	Lawrence E. Hendrix	Richard C. Knowlton
Carl Cratty	John E. Findley	Walter S. Hendzel	Raymond P. Krause
Donald Crooks	William K. Fite	Gustave L. Henricksen	Joseph Kritz
Cloyce V. Culver	Gerald J. Fitzgerald	Bernard R. Hill	Tellmer J. Kutlseth
Steve A. Cvaniga	David H. Flanders	Stephen E. Hoffman	Bernard B. Lacina
Edwin Dany	James C. Flippen	Theodore P. Hogstrom	Albert L. Lafferty
James A. Davis	Travis H. Flowers	Harley E. Holben	Melvin E. Laizure
Lonnie H. Davis	Frederick Frazy	Arthur M. Holm	Anthony A. Lamacki
Joe A. De Herrera	Joseph Gallo	Delbert B. Homer	Raymond T. Laurion
Elmer H. Dessert	Joe A. Gandara	George E. Hopkins, Jr.	Lawrence H. LeBar
Michael S. Destefano	William V. Garland	Joseph D. Horwity	Arthur W. Lechner, Jr.
Harlow L. Dicks	Clarence M. Garrison	John K. House	George E. Ledo
Russell W. Dimon	Clifford M. Gelnette	James Hubeny	Medore J. Leneau
Donald L. Dixon	John L. Gerst	John F. Hunt	Milton Levey
Harold Doan	Lawrence E. Gilbert	Dean E. Hunter	Casimer Lewandowski
Angelo V. Domenico	John A. Gilbertson	Leonard J. Hurst	Dwaine R. Lewis
John H. Domenico	William A. Goad	Preston M. Hutchinson	Leland L. Lewis
Lazaro J. Dominguez	Augustine L. Gomey	William B. Ide, Jr.	Floyd Loomis
Earl F. Donahue	Robert Goulet	Fred B. Jacobson	Leopoldo Lopey

Charles L. Loughrey
Juan Lucero
John Lysak
Robert W. MacGregor
Theodore C. Maciak
Frank B. MacIntosh
Raymond T. Majewski
Warren D. Mann
Robert R. Mannis
Victor Mark
Carl W. Martin
Ralph Marzucca
Frederick P. May, Jr.
Herbert W. McCarty
Raymond E. McClellan
J. V. McCord
Bert McCrandell
Arthur R. McEllen
James W. McGinnis
John W. McGuire
Edward F. McHugh
Donald R. McLeod
Robert W. Mead
Kenneth E. Means
Ervin H. Meeker
Robert B. Meeker
Delmer D. Meints
Howard W. Mesecher
William A. Meurer
Thaddeus S. Micek
Robert K. Mika
Delmar Mikesell
Herbert J. Miller
Lewis F. Miller
Warren C. Mitchell
Irving E. Moehrke
Correl W. Mommaerts
Wilbur G. Moore
William C. Nagel
Charles E. Nedrow
William G. Neff
Robert C. Nelson
Paul J. Niemi
William E. Noack
Warren J. Norrgard
Carl J. Nystrom
Daniel F. O'Leary

Glenn E. Olson
James T. Orfield
Jimmy Z. Ortiz
Donald W. Osenga
Bernard H. Oudeans
Eldon E. Palmer
Joseph Parijczuk
Dominic A. Pelowski
Emilio C. Perretti
Francis G. Peters
Walter M. Pietraszek
Leonard W. Pitlyk
Alton R. Place
John J. Plettner
Stephen D. Pogue
Ellsworth D. Pool
Robert F. Pooler
Ralph S. Prague
Glenn W. Proctor
Dwight E. Rabe
William E. Raines
Maurice A. Rath
Charles S. Ratzloff
William F. Regan
Edward A. Rekar
Emil F. Rizzi
Vito Rizzi
Werner M. Rondell
Leonard J. Root
Dominic Rosa
Victor A. Roskey
James H. Rusk
Darrell B. Rutherford
Stephen Ryfun
William J. Rymer
Herman W. Sacks
Robert H. St. Mary
Carroll P. Saley
Jose E. Sandoval
Fred E. Sayer
Harold J. Schaalma
John N. Schavilje
Johnie A. Schepers
Gaile H. Schirmer
Walter H. Schmidt
Robert G. Schrader
Alexander Schwabouer

Leonard L. Schwartz
Bruno Scodallaro
Gurnie D. Scott
Robert G. Scrutchfield
John T. Sells
Joseph Semas
Edward J. Senkeleski
Claude O. Senser
George W. Shaffer
Emil Singer
George Sinkevich, Jr.
Valerian W. Silban
Samuel M. Sliger
James F. Slattery
Abner H. Smith
James H. Smith
Richard H. Smith
Robert E. Smith
John A. Snodgrass
Casimer Soboleski
Alexander P. Socha
Robert K. Sorensen
Allen W. Stan
George Stark
William R. Steinke
William A. Steinman
Paul Stengel
Duane R. Stevenson
Otto C. Stonebraker
Robert C. Strejc
William M. Stuller
Donald W. Sullivan
Walter R. Sutliff
Kenneth D. Swanson
Frederick W. Tatro
Forrest H. Taylor, Jr.
Lawrence Tennity
Ted B. Theodorsen
Theodore Thompson
Moses A. Totty
Robert W. Tucker
Edmund J. Tumas
Joe A. Turner
Norman H. Uecker
Fred B. Underwood
Bonnie D. Valdez
Caterino Valles

John J. Van Horn
Glenn D. Van Slyke
Richard E. Varcoe
Charles W. Vaughn
Mack D. Vaughn
Duane D. Vegors
Adolfo Vela
Eugene C. Vest
Ricardo J. L. Vigil
Louis J. Vitale
Fermon Waggoner
William E. Walders
Francis F. Walker
Charles A. Warson
Maurice D. Wasmuth
Clarence J. Wassenberg
William E. Watkins
Charles H. Webber
Henry Weisoly
Lyle M. Wendorf
Frank L. Wever
Zenon M. Weyna
Albert T. Wheeldon
Francis E. White
Joe R. Whiteside
Clifford M. Wiksten
Emil H. Wildauer
Alfred P. Williams
Forrest E. Williams
Lewis D. Williams
Howard H. Willsey
Alan M. Wilson
Hall H. Wilson
Harold E. Wiltse
Edward G. Wokas
Crawford H. Wood
Gordon N. Wood
Graddie Woods
Wilbert L. Wuolo
Harold Yoblong
Harold A. Yuergens
Charles E. Young
Norman L. Zans
Arthur H. Zeigler
Louis Zifko
Stanley J. Zwlmanski
Theodore Zyhowski

COMPANY "C"

Vito L. Albanese
Carlos Alexander
Lester T. Alveshere
Axel J. Anderson
Edwin F. Anderson
Andrew J. Andrews
Paul L. Anstead
John A. Augustyniak
Joseph R. Ayottee
Kenneth L. Baldwin
Lionel E. Bates
Shirley D. Batron
Henry E. Baumdraher

Jack O. Beason
Linus G. Becker
Walteman V. Becker
Raymond F. Bedell
John Belive
Joseph A. Bernier
Joseph B. Bloomquist
Otto R. Bogner
Richard H. Brimmer
William L. Broyles
Bernard F. Brzyski
Cleveland D. Buckland
James J. Burke

Earl J. Burrell
John C. Byrd
Lanthon D. Camblin
Charles Capan
James R. Cardinelli
Verda L. Carney
Howard M. Case
George E. Casler
Glen W. Cassen
Paul E. Champagne
Alfred Chartrand
Frederick K. Classen
Raymond Clemmons

Carl T. Colaianni
Virgil E. Cole
Joseph W. Collahan
Clinton H. Comerford
Bruce E. Coons
Sam S. Corrado
James E. Coy
Cloyce V. Culver
John L. Davis, Jr.
Wayne S. Deal
Ralph C. Demarest
Elmer H. Dessert
John F. DeVito

(1) Company C. (2) Headquarters Platoon. (3 1st Platoon. (4) 2d Platoon.
(5) 3d Platoon.

Michael Di Bari	Robert G. Gideon	Walter Jarzynski	Daniel R. Lusk
Benjamin A. Di Bello	Leecoy S. Gilkison	George E. Jefferson	Dean R. Mack
Harlan L. Dicks	Guy W. Glanville	Floyd A. Johnson	Weikko E. Maki
Frank A. Dieboll	Alfred A. Glaser	Cerel M. Jones	John J. Marchel
Mike Dillman	John R. Gonacha	Clifford A. Jones	Thaddeus F. Marchel
Joseph Doiron	Howard V. Goodrow	Herbert H. Jones	Glen D. Marple
Edward S. Dolliver	Robert Goulet	Frank D. Jurenic	Dale L. McCartney
Bruno Dombrowski	Clarence Gower	Loren L. Kammerer	Francis M. McCown
John W. Domanski	Chester S. Gralewicz	Anton L. Kasprowicz	Harry E. McDaniel
Albert E. Donati, Jr.	John D. Green	George M. Kelley	John M. McDaniel
Raymond J. Droste	Jesse D. Guyer	Newell L. Kemp	Alex J. McRobb
William Dzwonkowski	Eino H. Haapala	Edward J. Kennedy	Julius J. Meyer
John W. Eck	Stanley C. Hahula	Kendall V. Kennedy	Edmond T. Mieszczur
Elmore P. Edwards	Wilburn Hailey	Walter L. Kennon	George W. Miklovic
Robert G. Emmert	Roger L. Hain	Peter H. Kern	George B. Miller
Alex Y. Epstein	Edwin R. Hanks	Guy Kinconon	John P. Miller
Daniel A. Fanning	James K. Harrington	Kenneth C. King	Wendell Miller
Clyde Y. Favinger	Robert F. Haury	Harold J. Kipfmiller	Joseph D. Montecarlo
Vincent J. Fazzino	Hugo Hedlund	George A. Klotz	George S. Montie, Jr.
Bertrand L. Feldmeier	Charles B. Haffner	Gerald L. Koch	Norris J. Morse
Earl G. Fesler	Harry J. Hendricks	Samuel Koch	John Mucci
John F. Fincher	Arnold M. Hendrickson	Richard E. Koelmel	Robert S. Myers
Thomas M. Fitzgerald	Carl W. Hibbs	Douglas A. Kohl	Otto H. Naegeli
Joe S. Fitzsimmons	Louis H. Hollenbeck	Sylvester P. Kozlowski	Vincent D. Nagle
Daniel J. Flaherty	Kenneth D. Holloway	Thaddeus F. Krajewski	Charles E. Nedrow
LeRoy Fonner	Raymond L. Horan	Alfred W. Kurck, Jr.	Charles L. Nehrbass
Richard H. Forbes	Charles R. Horsell	Clement F. Kryspin	William V. Nelson
Carl M. Friend	Dean E. Hunter	Bernard B. Lacina	James A. Nenart
Norbert J. Ganter	Robert B. Hurley	Edward G. Lankowski	Wilfrid J. O'Donnell
Melvin J. Gardner	George Hutchings	Rex A. Larabee	William H. Orr, Jr.
Henry P. Gawle	William B. Ide, Jr.	Dewey O. Leroux	Jimmy Z. Ortiz
Philip P. Gendron	Sumner L. Irrael	Salvadore Licavoli	Marvin L. Osgood
Walter G. Germann	Charles W. Jackson	William E. Losee	Amel E. Ott, Jr.
William R. Gibbons	Lawrence H. Jaros	Wilbur E. Ludlam	Gilbert T. Owens

James Owens	Mike A. Rios	Abner H. Smith	Albert Trujillo
Harold A. Parker	James L. Rizzo	Jesse J. Sneed	Leo Tucker
Victor P. Parrino	Oscar E. Roe	David L. Snow	Melvin Umphrey
Kenneth G. Perry	John Romero	Francis R. Sodee	John J. Van Horn
Chester L. Peters	Leonard J. Root	Joseph H. Sokola	Emil E. Varcolan
Arthur L. Peterson	Andy Rosa, Jr.	Eugene E. Sollie	Carl Veltri
Wesley J. Peterson	Victor A. Roskey	Orville J. Sorensen	Joseph A. Vermette
Orleen V. Piccirilli	Adolph J. Rosol	Glenn W. Spencer	James G. Vornberger
Stephen P. Pietrzak	Gerald M. Ryan	Charles H. Spires	Arthur J. Waldero
Roland C. Pilz	William J. Rymer	John Spreid	Francis F. Walker
Frank Placzek	Leonard F. Sages	Gene E. Stafford	Jack E. Wallington
Gwindlyn H. Platt	Earl J. Sanders	Albert R. Stauss	Frederic W. Walsh
Frank Popper, Jr.	Rafael Santiago	Paul Stengel	Robert D. Walther
William O. Porter	Chester W. Saunders	Duane R. Stevenson	Robert C. Washack
Warren K. Potter	John N. Schavilze	Harry Strauch	Maurice D. Wasmuth
Theodore A. Powell	Gaile H. Schirmer	Emil L. Strudle	Arthur J. Watson
Harold A. Prentice	Clarence R. Schmit	Harland A. Swager	Bennie B. Weber
Robert G. Pryor	John E. Scott	Elmer B. Swanson	Lyle M. Wendorf
William Przybylowicz	Carl S. Seaman	Irving H. Swarthout	Willard E. Whalen
Michaele T. Pulcini	Sheldon J. Shalett	Ernest W. Swindelhurst	Joe R. Whiteside
John P. Raffa	James E. Shanon	Marvin R. Sykes	Thomas E. Whitney
Toivo A. Rajala	Thomas L. Sheil	Joseph J. Tarasewicz	John J. Wielgus
Saturnino M. Ramos	Lloyd W. Shellenbarger	John W. Taylor	Charles E. Wilcox
Charles S. Ratzloff	Clarence W. Shultz	August R. Thaler	Charlie C. Williams
Michael J. Rawlings	Edward H. Sidell	Robert M. Thelen	Ira L. Williamson
Archie M. Reed	Samuel E. Siegel	Joseph L. Thomas	Clyde Wilson
Joseph E. Reynolds	Floyd R. Sievers	Donald A. Thompson	Harold E. Wiltse
Thomas J. Rhone	Levor D. Siglin	Earl L. Threlkeld	Robert K. Winter
William A. Rice	Clark R. Simon, Jr.	Clarence J. Tollard	Albert E. Wolluck
Raymond Richardson	Walter A. Skiba	Walter R. Travers	Wilbert L. Wuolo

Lawrence J. Yarmoska   Harold A. Yuergens

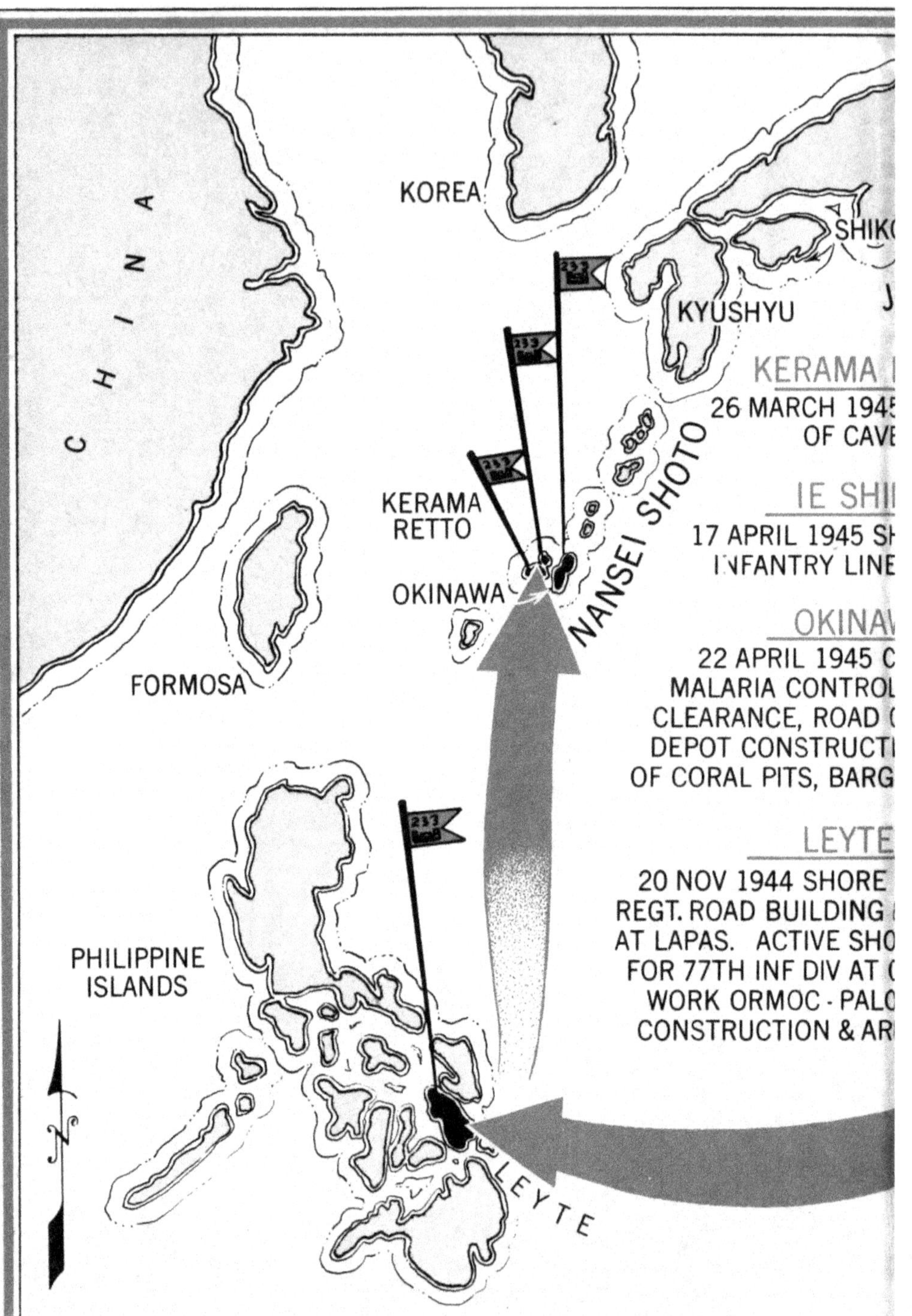

CHINA
KOREA
SHIKO
KYUSHYU
J
KERAMA
26 MARCH 1945
OF CAVE
IE SHI
17 APRIL 1945 SH
INFANTRY LINE
OKINAW
22 APRIL 1945 C
MALARIA CONTROL
CLEARANCE, ROAD
DEPOT CONSTRUCTI
OF CORAL PITS, BARG
LEYTE
20 NOV 1944 SHORE
REGT. ROAD BUILDING
AT LAPAS. ACTIVE SHO
FOR 77TH INF DIV AT
WORK ORMOC - PALO
CONSTRUCTION & AR
KERAMA
RETTO
OKINAWA
NANSEI SHOTO
FORMOSA
PHILIPPINE
ISLANDS
LEYTE
N

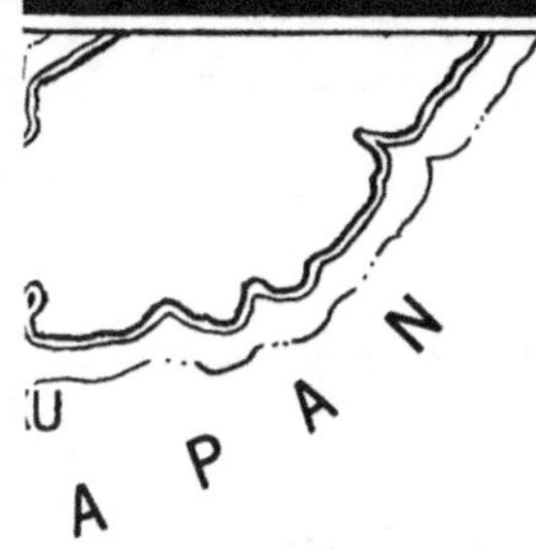
J A P A N

ACTIVITIES OF
233D ENGR (C) BN.
IN
PACIFIC THEATRE OF OPERATIONS
28 MARCH 1944 — 22 JUNE 1945

:TTO
LOSING

RE PARTY
UPPORT

JSE WAYS,
CARGO AREA
NSTRUCTION,
, OPERATION
CONSTRUCTION

RTY 307 INF
MAINTENANCE
PARTY WORK
AOC, BRIDGE
PON, RAMP
CLEARANCE

MARIANAS

GUAM

GUAM
21 JULY 1944 SHORE PARTY
OPERATIONS FOR 307 INF
ROAD BUILDING & MAINTENANCE
BAILEY BRIDGE TRAINING

OAHU
28 MARCH 1944 AMPHIBIOUS
TRAINING, JUNGLE TRAINING,
ROAD BUILDING, CAMP CONSTRUCTION
KAHUKU ARMY AIR BASE

SCALE:1/2″= 100 MILES

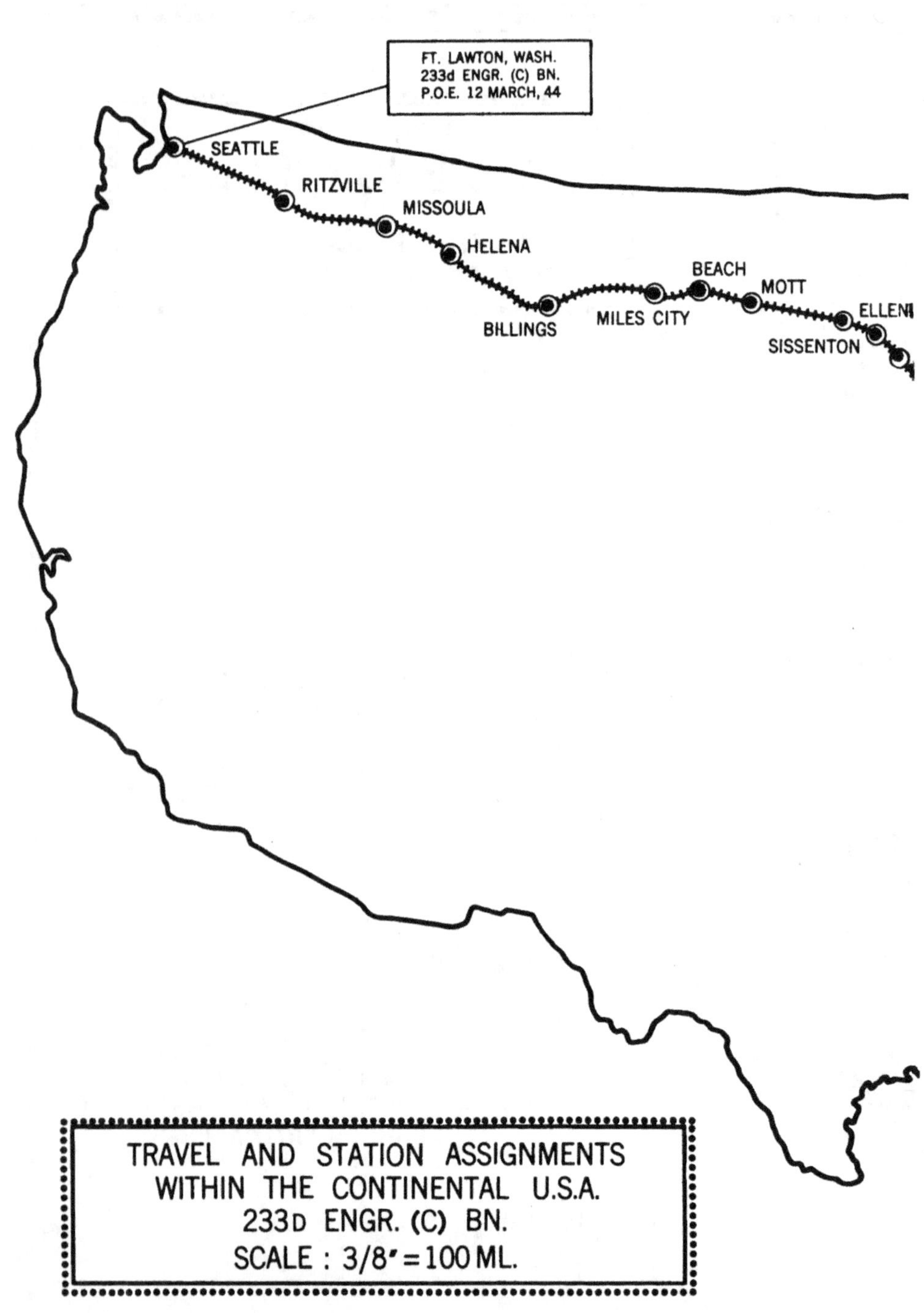

FT. LAWTON, WASH.
233d ENGR. (C) BN.
P.O.E. 12 MARCH, 44
SEATTLE
RITZVILLE
MISSOULA
HELENA
BILLINGS
MILES CITY
BEACH
MOTT
SISSENTON
ELLEN[
TRAVEL AND STATION ASSIGNMENTS
WITHIN THE CONTINENTAL U.S.A.
233D ENGR. (C) BN.
SCALE : 3/8" = 100 ML.

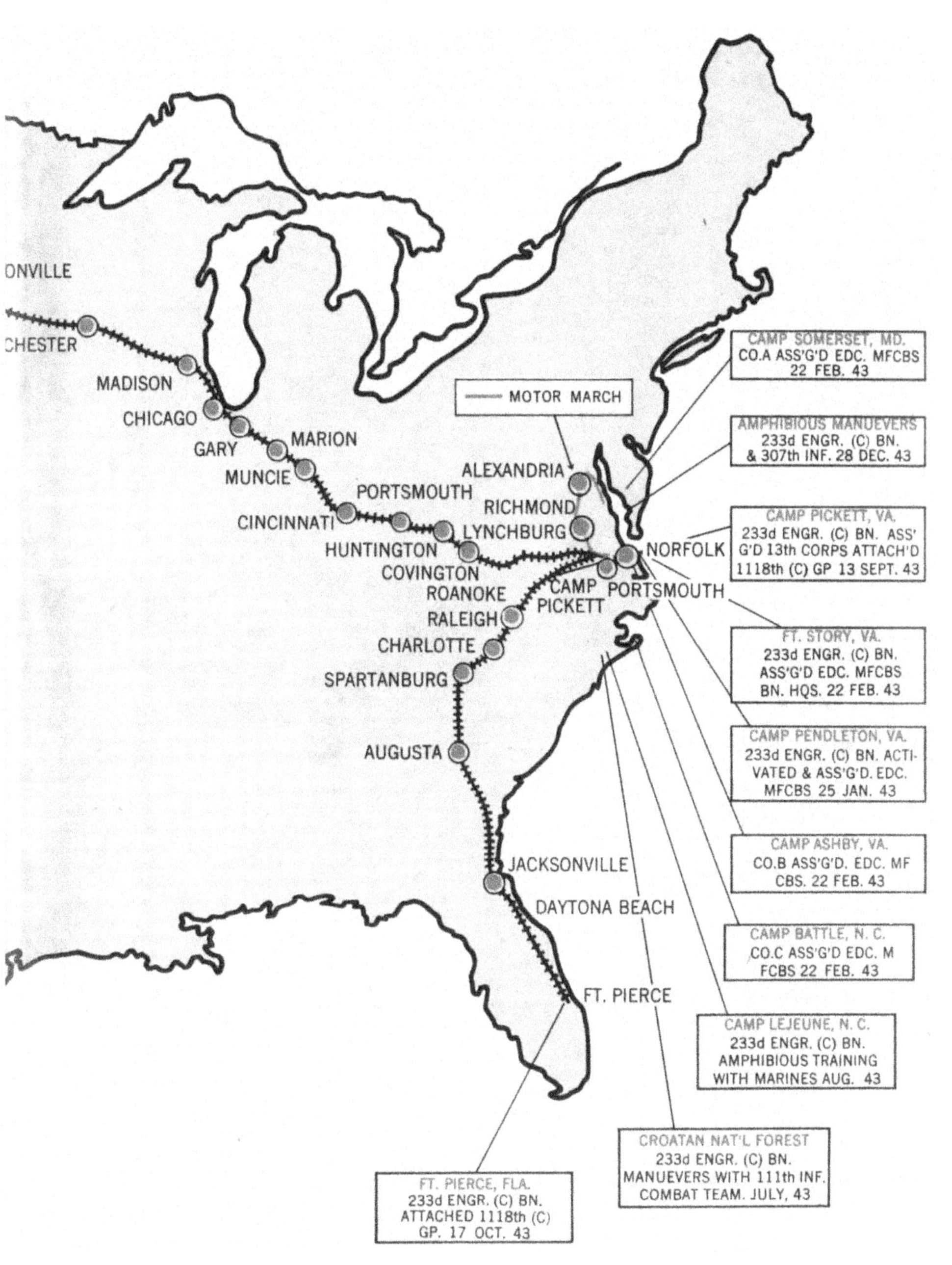
ONVILLE
CHESTER
MADISON
CHICAGO
GARY
MARION
MUNCIE
PORTSMOUTH
CINCINNATI
ALEXANDRIA
RICHMOND
LYNCHBURG
HUNTINGTON
NORFOLK
COVINGTON
ROANOKE
CAMP PICKETT
PORTSMOUTH
RALEIGH
CHARLOTTE
SPARTANBURG
AUGUSTA
JACKSONVILLE
DAYTONA BEACH
FT. PIERCE
MOTOR MARCH
CAMP SOMERSET, MD.
CO.A ASS'G'D EDC. MFCBS
22 FEB. 43
AMPHIBIOUS MANUEVERS
233d ENGR. (C) BN.
& 307th INF. 28 DEC. 43
CAMP PICKETT, VA.
233d ENGR. (C) BN. ASS'
G'D 13th CORPS ATTACH'D
1118th (C) GP 13 SEPT. 43
FT. STORY, VA.
233d ENGR. (C) BN.
ASS'G'D EDC. MFCBS
BN. HQS. 22 FEB. 43
CAMP PENDLETON, VA.
233d ENGR. (C) BN. ACTI-
VATED & ASS'G'D. EDC.
MFCBS 25 JAN. 43
CAMP ASHBY, VA.
CO.B ASS'G'D. EDC. MF
CBS. 22 FEB. 43
CAMP BATTLE, N. C.
CO.C ASS'G'D EDC. M
FCBS 22 FEB. 43
CAMP LEJEUNE, N. C.
233d ENGR. (C) BN.
AMPHIBIOUS TRAINING
WITH MARINES AUG. 43
CROATAN NAT'L FOREST
233d ENGR. (C) BN.
MANUEVERS WITH 111th INF.
COMBAT TEAM. JULY, 43
FT. PIERCE, FLA.
233d ENGR. (C) BN.
ATTACHED 1118th (C)
GP. 17 OCT. 43

9 798886 903632